Standard Letters in Architectural Practice

Also of interest

The Architect in Practice
Seventh Edition
David Chappell & Christopher J. Willis
0–632–02267–1

Standard Letters for Building Contractors
Second Edition
David Chappell
0–632–03452–1

The JCT Design and Build Contract
David Chappell & Vincent Powell-Smith
0–632–02081–4

In preparation

Building Contract Claims
Third Edition
Vincent Powell-Smith, John Sims & David Chappell
0–632–03646–X

Standard Letters in Architectural Practice

Second Edition

David Chappell
BA (Hons Arch), MA(Arch), MA (Law), PhD, RIBA
Architect and Contracts Consultant
Chappell-Marshall Limited

Blackwell
Science

© D. M. Chappell 1987, 1994

Blackwell Science Ltd
Editorial Offices:
Osney Mead, Oxford OX2 0EL
25 John Street, London WC1N 2BL
23 Ainslie Place, Edinburgh EH3 6AJ
238 Main Street, Cambridge,
  Massachusetts 02142, USA
54 University Street, Carlton,
  Victoria 3053, Australia

Other Editorial Offices:
Arnette Blackwell SA
1, rue de Lille
75007 Paris
France

Blackwell Wissenschafts-Verlag GmbH
Kurfürstendamm 57
10707 Berlin
Germany

Blackwell MZV
Feldgasse 13
A-1238 Wien
Austria

DISTRIBUTORS

Marston Book Services Ltd
PO Box 87
Oxford OX2 0DT
(*Orders*: Tel: 01865 791155
        Fax: 01865 791927
        Telex: 837515)

USA
Blackwell Science, Inc.
238 Main Street
Cambridge, MA 02142
(*Orders*: Tel: 800 759-6102
                617 876-7000)

Canada
Oxford University Press
70 Wynford Drive
Don Mills
Ontario M3C 1J9
(*Orders*: Tel: 416 441-2941)

Australia
Blackwell Science Pty Ltd
54 University Street
Carlton, Victoria 3053
(*Orders*: Tel: 03 347-5552)

A catalogue record for this book is available
from the British Library

ISBN 0–632–03451–3

Library of Congress
Cataloging in Publication Data
is available

First Edition published by
  The Architectural Press 1987
Second Edition published by
  Blackwell Science Ltd 1994

Set by DP Photosetting, Aylesbury, Bucks
Printed and bound in Great Britain by
Hartnolls Ltd, Bodmin, Cornwall

Contents

7 Bills of Quantities   **113**
Letters

8 Tender Action   **116**
Letters

Preface for Second Edition

The first edition of this book was very successful and I have been pleased on several occasions to find a letter based on one of the standard formats among the correspondence in a file I have been asked to examine. This kind of unsolicited evidence that the book is useful makes the hard work of putting it together worthwhile.

All the JCT Amendments have been taken into account including Amendment 13 to JCT 80, Amendment 6 to IFC 84, Amendment MW8 to MW 80 and the 1990 revision of GC/Works/1 edition 3. In order to keep the size and price under control and to increase its usefulness, this edition has discarded references to the ACA form of contract in favour of the increasingly popular CD 81 (including Amendment 7) design and build form in which the architect may act for employer or contractor and sometimes, although not at the same time please, for both. This latter is termed 'consultant switch', but its intricacies are outside the scope of a book of standard letters. Reference to the new RIBA Standard Form of Agreement for the Appointment of an Architect 1992 (SFA92) have replaced the RIBA Architect's Appointment 1982.

Every letter has been reviewed and if deemed appropriate in the light of experience or subsequent case law, the wording has been amended. Some letters have been omitted and new ones have been inserted and the clause references have been changed as necessary. The typeface of the letters has been improved so that it is easier to distinguish between the text and directory notes. Explanatory text is still kept to a minimum in front of each section. It is hoped that the letters, with their titles and text notes, are self-explanatory.

My thanks to Professor Vincent Powell-Smith who kindly allowed me to use some of his material in the first edition, some of which has survived; to Julia Burden for patience when the heavy workload associated with starting a new consultancy practice threatened to delay the completion of this book unconscionably; to Sue Moore for her editorial skills in producing several books for me, of which this is the latest; and to my wife Margaret as always.

DAVID CHAPPELL
Chappell-Marshall Limited
176A Easterly Road
Leeds
LS8 3AD
May 1994

Introduction

This book is written for architects although other members of the construction industry may find it useful. It is a book of standard letters – the sort of letters that have to be written time after time. An attempt has been made to include all the common situations which an architect will encounter when dealing with a project. It is, of course, an impossible task, and it is inevitable that some situations suitable for a standard letter fail to appear. I should be glad to receive, care of the publishers, any suggestions for standard letters for inclusion in a later edition.

These letters are not intended to relieve the user of the necessity of understanding the contracts; they are simply to relieve the tedium of composing letters for fairly standard situations. In order to reduce the large number of letters to manageable proportions, they have been divided into sections which follow the RIBA Plan of Work. Letters have been arranged in what appears to be a logical order.

Unless otherwise stated, all letters are suitable for use with The Standard Form of Building Contract (JCT 80), The Standard Form with Contractor's Design (CD 81), The Intermediate Form (IFC 84), The Agreement for Minor Building Works (MW 80) and the General Conditions of Contract for Building and Civil Engineering (GC/Works/1 edition 3). Where different contracts require a different letter, a note indicates the fact. Although, in general, each letter deals with a separate item for the sake of simplicity, it is appreciated that such items are in practice often gathered into one letter. Standard items already available elsewhere, such as standard forms of tender and certificates of various kinds, are not included.

The following points should be borne in mind when using this book:

- Every letter should have a heading giving the project title. Headings have been omitted for simplicity's sake.
- The masculine gender has been used throughout, but 'he' may be taken to mean 'she', 'his' to mean 'hers', etc.
- Variants are usually given in the same letter, but if it is more convenient or less confusing or an important letter is concerned, separate alternative letters are given and indicated by adding a,b,c, etc, to the letter number.
- The terms 'architect', 'client' or 'employer' have been used throughout for consistency, but it should be noted that, when using GC/Works/1, the employer is termed the 'authority' and the architect is termed the 'PM'. Letters normally written by the architect under other forms of contract, are sometimes written by the authority under GC/Works/1.
- When using CD 81, the term 'architect' should be read as 'employer's agent' and it is assumed that the architect is taking this role. The complexities of 'consultant switch' have proved too much to handle in a book of this kind. That does not mean that some of the letters cannot be used in these circumstances, but especial care must be taken.
- It has been assumed that the Supplementary Provisions have been used with CD 81.

A word of warning. Standard letters can be very useful, but they can also be dangerous if they are used without thought. Always consider carefully whether a standard letter is really appropriate in the circumstances. If in doubt, seek advice.

1 Inception

The letters in this stage are concerned with your initial relations with your client, the appointment of consultants in various ways and the use of sub-contractors in a design capacity together with the difficult question of warranties or duty of care agreements.

It is absolutely vital that you confirm all the details of your agreement with your client. Because these matters become commonplace and almost routine, they are sometimes forgotten. Although there are instances when a special letter must be written, standard letters are useful in conjunction with other standard documents such as the RIBA Standard Form of Agreement for the Appointment of an Architect 1992 (SFA92)

It is wise to ensure that your client directly employs all consultants. The standard clauses in SFA92 will then afford you protection if a consultant is negligent.

You may not delegate design work without the client's express authority. In addition, you should ensure that the client enters into direct agreement with sub-contractors carrying out any design work in order to provide the client with a remedy for failure of the sub-contractor's design. Such agreements are commonly termed 'warranties' and architects are usually requested to enter into a warranty in favour of the employer or a funder and assignable. Without such warranties, the architect's liabilities in tort for defective design are likely to be minimal in practice. It is, therefore undesirable to sign a warranty, but commercial pressures may make refusal difficult.

Letter 1
To client, if asked to tender on fees

Dear Sir

Thank you for your letter of the [*insert date*].

I am pleased to hear that you are considering my appointment as architect for the above project. The **RIBA** Code of Professional Conduct lays down criteria which I must satisfy before quoting a fee. These relate to the nature and scope of the project and the precise services required.

May I suggest that you telephone me to arrange a suitable date and time to discuss the project? A copy of the Standard Form of Agreement for the Appointment of an Architect (SFA92) is enclosed for general information and to enable you to form an idea of the services you will require. If appointed, it will form the basis of our agreement.

I look forward to meeting you.

Yours faithfully

Letter 2
To prospective client, offering services

Dear Sir

I was interested to hear that you intend to   [*insert nature of development*]. I do not know whether you have already commissioned an architect for the work. If not, this letter is to let you know that I would be delighted to discuss the project with you.

A copy of my illustrated brochure is enclosed and I hope you will find it of interest. You will see that this practice is experienced in carrying out work of the kind you appear to have in mind.

If you consider that a meeting would be mutually beneficial, please let me know.

Yours faithfully

Letter 3
To client, setting out terms of appointment

Dear Sir

I refer to our conversation/your letter [*delete as appropriate*] of the [*insert date*] regarding my appointment as architect for the above project. I am happy to accept this commission.

I confirm that the terms and conditions which will apply to the project are those set out in the RIBA Standard Form of Agreement for the Appointment of an Architect (SFA92), two copies of which are enclosed. They are completed in accordance with the terms we discussed. I should be pleased if you would complete the documents in the spaces indicated by yellow stickers and pencil crosses and return one copy to me. The other copy is for your retention and information.

Please check that the services and basis of fee calculation is satisfactory. If you have any queries, please do not hesitate to ask me for clarification.

Yours faithfully

Letter 4

To client, requesting payment in advance

Dear Sir

Thank you for your letter of the [*insert date*] instructing me to carry out architectural services in connection with the above project.

I should be pleased to visit you/see you at this office [*delete as appropriate*] to discuss your detailed requirements and my terms of appointment. I would ask for a payment on account of [*insert percentage*] of the estimated total fees* at the time of signing the agreement between us.

A copy of the RIBA Standard Form of Agreement for the Appointment of an Architect (SFA92) is enclosed. After you have had the opportunity to examine it, perhaps you will telephone me to arrange a convenient date and time for our meeting.

Yours faithfully

[* *You may find it prevents dispute if you insert an actual sum instead of a percentage*]

Letter 5
To client, regarding other architects engaged on the work

Dear Sir

In order to comply with the RIBA Code of Professional
Conduct, I am required to make reasonable enquiries to discover
if you have previously engaged any other architect on this
project.

If another architect has been involved at any time, perhaps you
will let me have his/her [*delete as appropriate*] name and
address so that I can inform him/her [*delete as appropriate*] that
I am now acting for you.

Yours faithfully

Letter 6
To client, if architect asked to sign a warranty

Dear Sir

Thank you for your letter of the *[insert date]* with which you enclosed a form of warranty for signature.

There is nothing in the Standard Form of Agreement for the Appointment of an Architect 1992/the terms of engagement governing my appointment *[delete as appropriate]* which obliges me to enter into a warranty agreement. I am sure you understand that if I was to execute such a warranty, the scope of my potential liability would be substantially increased.

However, I appreciate that a warranty agreement is a valuable commodity, particularly where sale or full repairing lease is concerned. Therefore, I am prepared to enter into a warranty in appropriate terms on payment of a small additional fee as consideration. A copy of a simple standard form of warranty is enclosed and I should be pleased if you would let me know if its terms are acceptable. I am afraid that they are not negotiable in this instance. My fee would be *[insert fee required which should be more than nominal]*.

Yours faithfully

Letter 7

To other architect, regarding former engagement

Dear Sir

I have been approached by [*insert name of client*] to undertake the above project.

I understand that you were engaged on this project at one time and you should take this letter as notice in accordance with principle 3, rule 3.5 of the RIBA Code of Professional Conduct.

If you have any comments, I should be pleased to receive them.

Yours faithfully

Letter 8

To client, if former architect notifies some problem

Dear Sir

I have been informed by [*insert name of former architect*] that [*insert nature of problem*].

Clearly this is not my direct concern but, entirely at your discretion, you may wish to appraise me of the full circumstances.

[*In some circumstances it may be wise to add the following:*]

In this instance, however, and without passing any comment on the respective liabilities under the previous engagement, I will require a payment on account of [*insert amount*] before I undertake this commission.

Yours faithfully

Letter 9

To client, regarding early appointment of consultants

Dear Sir

The appointment of consultants is advisable at this stage in order to prevent abortive work and ensure that you obtain the very best value for money.

In accordance with clause 4.1.3 of the conditions of the Standard Form of Agreement for the Appointment of an Architect, I confirm that the following consultants should be appointed to provide the services noted:

[*List the consultants and services*]

Subject to your agreement, I will approach each firm and negotiate the extent of service required and the fees payable. The appointments can be finalised at a series of meetings at which I will be present to give you general advice and clarification.

I should be pleased to have your instructions to proceed with the course of action outlined above.

Yours faithfully

Letter 10
To client, if he queries early appointment of consultants

Dear Sir

Thank you for your letter of the *[insert date]* and I note that you do not wish to appoint consultants at this stage.

The erection of a modern building is a very complex process. At one time it was possible for an architect to deal with every aspect of a large contract without assistance from anyone other than his own office staff. Advances in technology, materials and building science, however, render such an undertaking impractical for one professional.

Consultants are a necessity on this project; they are listed in Schedule Four of the Standard Form of Agreement for the Appointment of an Architect. Appointment at this stage will be most economical in the long term and you will have the benefit of their advice from the beginning of the design process. Not only would delay in appointment be against my direct advice, it would result in additional fees chargeable as a result of my abortive work. Such fees would be likely to be substantial. I should be grateful if you would give the matter serious consideration and let me have your instructions within, say, the next week.

Yours faithfully

Letter 11
To client, enclosing draft for appointment of consultants

Dear Sir

I refer to the series of meetings on the [*insert date*] when we met each consultant proposed for this project and we finalised details of the appointment.

I enclose the following:

1.   Two copies of the agreement which I have received in respect of each consultant. I have checked them and they correspond with the terms discussed at our meeting.
2.   A draft letter which I have prepared for you to send with the completed agreement to each consultant.

Please satisfy yourself that the agreements are in accordance with your requirements, then complete them in the spaces indicated and return one copy of each to the appropriate consultant. The remaining copies should be retained for your own reference.

Yours faithfully

Letter 12
Client to consultant [*draft prepared by architect*]

Dear Sir

The architect has forwarded to me two copies of the agreement for consultancy work which you have prepared in respect of the above project.

I have examined the above documents and I return one copy duly completed as requested. Please note that the architect will be responsible for the co-ordination and integration of your services into the overall design and I expect you to co-operate fully in this respect. To avoid confusion, I should be grateful if you would not report directly to me unless there is some very pressing reason.

Yours faithfully

Letter 13
To client, if consultants' agreements are complex

Dear Sir

I refer to the series of meetings on the [*insert date*] when we met each consultant proposed for this project and discussed details of appointment.

I have now received copies of agreements in respect of each consultant. Each agreement is quite complex and, in my view, expert advice is required. I should be pleased to have your agreement to approach [*insert name*] on your behalf to seek advice and practical assistance in ensuring that the agreements to be used for each consultant properly reflect the appropriate duties and that there are no problems with the interaction of one agreement with another.

If you agree, I will obtain details of fee rates for your approval before proceeding.

Yours faithfully

Letter 14
To client, if client wishes architect to appoint consultants

Dear Sir

Thank you for your letter of the [*insert date*] from which I understand that you wish me to appoint the consultants for this project through my office.

It is, of course, perfectly possible to do as you suggest, but it would be against my advice. It is my responsibility to co-ordinate and integrate all consultancy services, however appointed.

Consultancy fees are unaffected by the method of appointment. However, the normal practice in construction projects is that the client appoints his own consultants. By doing so, you have direct access to the other professionals as the work proceeds and, of course, direct recourse to them for any problems which may arise.

I strongly urge you to reconsider and I look forward to hearing from you on this matter within the next few days to avoid delay.

Yours faithfully

Letter 15
To client, if architect is to appoint consultants

Dear Sir

Thank you for your letter of the *[insert date]* in which you instruct me that I am to engage the services of consultants on your behalf. The matter will be put in hand.

I should draw your attention to clause 4.1.7 of the Standard Form of Agreement for the Appointment of an Architect, a copy of which is already in your possession, which provides that you will hold each consultant however appointed responsible for the competence and performance of the services to be performed by him and for the general inspection and execution of such work. For the avoidance of doubt, clause 4.1.7 will apply to all consultants engaged by me on your instructions.

Yours faithfully

Letter 16
To client, if architect wishes to appoint consultants

Dear Sir

On projects of this nature, it is my usual practice to appoint consultants to deal with that part of the work not normally within the range of services provided by the architect. Clause 4.1.1 of the conditions of the Standard Form of Agreement for the Appointment of an Architect refers.

May I have your agreement to the following appointments and services to be provided and the additional fees payable, such fees to be appropriate to the relevant consultancy.

[*List consultants and services*]

I should draw your attention to clause 4.1.7 of the conditions which provides that you will hold each consultant however appointed responsible for the competence and performance of the services to be performed by him and for the general inspection and execution of such work. For the avoidance of doubt, clause 4.1.7 will apply to all consultants engaged by me.

Yours faithfully

Letter 17
To consultant, seeking indemnity

Dear Sir

I refer to the recent discussions regarding your employment as consultant for [*identify the services*] on the above project.

Before a formal contract of engagement can be drawn up, I require you to provide me with proof that you carry and will continue to carry suitable and adequate professional indemnity insurance. Please signify your willingness to indemnify me against any liability, loss, expense or claims of any kind whatsoever in respect of the competence, general inspection and performance of the work entrusted to you.

Yours faithfully

Letter 18
To client if consultancy services to be provided by the architect

Dear Sir

On projects of this nature, it would be normal practice for the architect to recommend the appointment of consultants for particular aspects of the work. Clause 4.1.1 of the conditions of the Standard Form of Agreement for the Appointment of an Architect refers. The following services can be provided by my office and I should be pleased to have your agreement to such provision, and to the additional fees which will be appropriate to the relevant consultancy.

[*List the consultancy services to be provided*]

Yours faithfully

Letter 19

To client, suggesting the use of a supplier or sub-contractor in a design
capacity

Dear Sir

I should be pleased if you would signify your agreement in
principle to the use of the following specialist firms to carry out
design work in addition to supplying goods and executing work
in relation to specific portions of this project. I write in
accordance with clause 4.2.2 of the conditions of the Standard
Form of Agreement for the Appointment of an Architect.

[*List specialists and the work to be designed by each*]

The arrangement is quite normal in construction projects and
generally arises because these firms have a particular expertise
or patented systems proven in use over a number of years. In
the instances I have in mind it is neither practicable nor
economic to commission consultant's designs for execution by the
main contractor. The design work in question will, of course, be
excluded from consultants' fees and there is a system of
warranties and agreements to protect your interests in the event
of a design failure.

On receipt of your agreement, I will prepare a summary of my
proposals for your approval.

Yours faithfully

Letter 20
To client, regarding lists of firms to design and supply/execute

---

Dear Sir

I refer to my letter of the [*insert date*] and your reply of the [*insert date*] approving the use of specialist firms in a design capacity.

I propose that the following firms be invited to tender for the parts of the project as indicated:

[*List parts of project and the firms proposed*]

Please let me have your approval or observations so that I can begin the preparation of the necessary documentation without delay.

Yours faithfully

Letter 21
To client, regarding lists of firms to supply

Dear Sir

I should be pleased if you would signify your agreement to the following list of firms which I propose to invite to tender for the supply only of goods as follows:

[*List goods and the firms proposed*]

Please let me have your approval or observations so that I can begin to prepare the necessary documentation without delay.

Yours faithfully

Letter 22

To client, if a relatively new material or process is proposed

Dear Sir

I am writing to confirm our recent conversation regarding the use of [*insert name of material or process*].

The material/process [*delete as appropriate*] has only been in use for [*insert period*], but so far it appears to be successful. I have written to the manufacturers on your behalf explaining the proposed use and, as might be expected, they are entirely reassuring. They have put that reassurance in the form of a letter and expressed their willingness to complete a form of warranty in your favour. I have also received favourable comments from [*insert names of appropriate national or international technical organisations*] and copies of all correspondence is enclosed with this letter.

There is always a risk in using relatively untried materials or processes and, therefore, the final decision must be yours. However, I believe that the risk is within acceptable limits in this instance and there is no other material/process [*delete as appropriate*] which offers so many advantages. I should be pleased to have your decision not later than [*insert date*]. If you require any further advice on the matter, please do not hesitate to telephone me.

Yours faithfully

2 Feasibility

During this stage, you will be busy collecting information, and this is reflected by the letters which follow. You will make initial approaches to a number of authorities including the planning authority.

On small jobs, it is unlikely that you will produce a formal report, but remember that a carefully structured report is far better than a letter running into three or four pages. The author's *Report Writing for Architects* (1989) 2nd edn, Legal Studies & Services (Publishing) Ltd, provides many useful formats to assist in the production of clear and comprehensive reports in architectural practice.

A problem which sometimes arises during this or later stages is that the client wishes to proceed without the delays associated with obtaining all the necessary approvals. From the client's point of view, this can save time and money, but if the approvals are withheld, you will wish to claim your fees for abortive work.

Letter 23
To members of the design team, arranging meeting

Dear Sir

There will be a meeting of the design team for the above project at [*insert time*] on [*insert date*] at this office/on site [*delete as appropriate*]. I should be pleased if you would arrange to attend.

[*Add one or more of the following sentences as appropriate:*]

The meeting will be expected to last [*insert period*].

Sandwiches will be provided.

An agenda is attached to this letter.

Yours faithfully

Letter 24
To client, regarding site survey

Dear Sir

I confirm your instructions by telephone on the [*insert date*] to carry out a site survey complete with measurements and levels.

This work is additional to my normal services and extra fees and expenses will be chargeable on a time basis as indicated in Schedule Three of the Standard Form of Agreement for the Appointment of an Architect.

Yours faithfully

Letter 25
To client, before carrying out a site survey

Dear Sir

Before I carry out a survey of the above site, it is essential that I satisfy myself regarding the limits of your ownership. Such matters are frequently obscure, but they may have a crucial effect on the project.

A sketch plan is enclosed on which are noted the principal features: walls, roads, adjacent buildings, etc. I should be pleased if you would indicate the precise extent of your ownership, including the ownership of boundaries, by drawing a red line around the site and returning the sketch to me as soon as possible. Please show dimensions if available.

If the plan attached to your title deeds shows all this information clearly, please let me know where I can examine it. If you are in any doubt about your ownership, I advise you to ask your solicitor to indicate the boundaries for you.

Yours faithfully

Letter 26
To client, if requested to help in boundary negotiations

Dear Sir

Thank you for your letter of the [*insert date*].

I will be happy to assist in negotiations with adjoining owners in order to fix site boundaries. It will be in your own best interests if your own solicitor takes charge of the negotiations and I am present to advise.

This is an additional service [*insert, if appropriate: 'to the services already agreed in the Standard Form of Agreement for the Appointment of an Architect 1992'*] and an additional fee at the rate of [*insert amount*] per hour is chargeable and I should be pleased to have your agreement.

Please ask your solicitor to telephone me directly to arrange a meeting.

Yours faithfully

Letter 27
To client, if problem encountered during survey

Dear Sir

I refer to our telephone conversation of the [*insert date*].

During my survey of the above property, it was discovered that [*insert a clear and concise description of the problem*].

In view of the implications and the effect upon the project, it is desirable that I meet you on site urgently. [*Add, if appropriate:*] I will invite [*insert name of consultant or contractor*] to be present to facilitate an immediate decision.

I will telephone you during the next day or so when I have made the necessary arrangements.

Yours faithfully

Letter 28
To geotechnical specialists, enquiring about soil survey

Dear Sir

I act as architect for the above development. My client is
[*insert name*].

My client has authorised me to seek quotations for the carrying
out of a ground investigation on the site.

The development will consist of [*insert brief description of the
size and character of the project*]. The design programme is
[*insert key dates*] and, therefore, the ground investigation must
be complete and in my hands by [*insert date*].

Please let me have details of the investigations you would carry
out and their cost. You will be expected to include for all
necessary work and attendance, protection of the public and
property and take out insurances and indemnify my client against
any claims arising from your occupation of or work on the site.
Site plan number [*insert number*] is enclosed for your
information.

Yours faithfully

Letter 29
To British Coal, requesting preliminary information

Dear Sir

I act as architect for the above development. My client is [*insert name*].

Two copies of the site plan number [*insert number*] and a general location plan of the area are enclosed. I should be pleased if you would inform me if this site is likely to be affected by your operations, past, present or projected. The proposed development is expected to be [*describe general character of the building including number of storeys*].

I enclose your fee in the sum of [*insert amount*].

Please consider this as notice on behalf of the building owner in accordance with the notice requirements of the Coal Mining Subsidence Act 1991, section 34(2)(a).

Yours faithfully

Copy: Client

Letter 30
To British Telecom, requesting preliminary information

Dear Sir

I act as architect for the above development. My client is
[*insert name*].

Two copies of the site plan number [*insert number*] are
enclosed. I should be pleased if you would examine it and let
me have the following information:

[*Delete as appropriate from the following:*]

1.   The position and depth below ground or height above
       ground of all telephone cables and services and the
       position of all poles or other equipment on or adjacent to
       the site.
2.   Any contribution to the cost of service which may be
       required from my client.
3.   Requirements with regard to service positions and inlet
       ducts.
4.   Any other special requirements.

Yours faithfully

Letter 31
To electricity supplier, requesting preliminary information

Dear Sir

I act as architect for the above development. My client is
[*insert name*].

Two copies of the site plan number [*insert number*] are
enclosed. I should be pleased if you would examine it and let
me have the following information:

[*Delete as appropriate from the following:*]

1. The position, size and depth of all electricity mains and
    known services on or adjacent to the site.
2. The amount of contribution to the cost which will be
    required from my client.
3. Requirements with regard to metering and inlet ducts.
4. Any other special requirements.

Yours faithfully

Letter 32

To gas supplier, requesting preliminary information

Dear Sir

I act as architect for the above development. My client is [*insert name*].

Two copies of the site plan number [*insert number*] are enclosed. I should be pleased if you would examine it and let me have the following information:

[*Delete as appropriate from the following:*]

1. The position, size and depth of all gas mains and known services on or adjacent to the site.
2. The amount of contribution to the cost of supply which will be required from my client.
3. Requirements with regard to metering and inlet ducts.
4. Any other special requirements.

Yours faithfully

Letter 33

To water supplier, requesting preliminary information

Dear Sir

I act as architect for the above development. My client is
[*insert name*].

Two copies of site plan number [*insert number*] are enclosed. I
should be pleased if you would examine it and let me have the
following information:

[*Delete as appropriate from the following:*]

1. The position, size and depth of all water mains and
   known services on or adjacent to the site.
2. The anticipated water pressure in the proposed supply.
3. The amount of contribution to the cost which will be
   required from my client.
4. Whether water metering is required.
5. Water storage requirements.
6. Local water regulations.

Yours faithfully

Letter 34
To drainage authority, requesting preliminary information

Dear Sir

I act as architect for the above development. My client is
[*insert name*].

Two copies of site plan number [*insert number*] are enclosed. I
should be pleased if you would examine it and let me have the
following information:

[*Delete as appropriate from the following:*]

1.   Positions, sizes, inverts and flow of all surface water and
       foul sewers on or adjacent to the site.
2.   System of drainage connection required and whether the
       authority wishes to carry out this part of the work.
3.   System of foul and surface water drainage from the site.
4.   Any particular requirements with regard to drainage in
       this area.
5.   Specification requirements.
6.   Any unusual site conditions such as flooding or
       surcharging of sewers.

Yours faithfully

Letter 35
To highway authority, requesting preliminary information

Dear Sir

I act as architect for the above development. My client is
[*insert name*].

Two copies of the site plan number [*insert number*] are
enclosed. I should be grateful if you would examine it and let
me have the following information: [*Delete as appropriate from
the following:*]

1.   The position of any future motorway schemes which
      might affect the site or which are proposed in the vicinity
      of the site.
2.   The position of any future highway schemes which might
      affect the site or which are proposed in the vicinity of the
      site.
3.   The position of any building or improvement lines,
      existing or proposed, which might affect the site.
4.   Acceptable positions for ingress to and egress from the
      site.
5.   It is hoped to complete the development by [*insert date*]
      and I should be pleased to receive a copy of your highway
      specification which will be current at that date.
6.   Details of any further operations which might affect this
      development.

Yours faithfully

Letter 36
To National Power, requesting preliminary information

Dear Sir

I act as architect for the above development. My client is
[*insert name*].

Two copies of the site plan number [*insert number*] are
enclosed. I should be pleased if you would examine it and let
me know if you have any equipment on or adjacent to the site or
any proposals for the future which might affect the site.

Yours faithfully

Letter 37

To client, regarding fees for planning applications

Dear Sir

I anticipate being in a position to make application for outline/full [*delete as appropriate*] planning permission on the [*insert date*]. All planning authorities are required to charge fees in accordance with a schedule of charges.

I have calculated the fee payable in respect of this application from the authority's published scale of charges as [*insert amount*] and I should be pleased to receive your cheque for this amount which you should draw in favour of [*insert name of planning authority*]. Final confirmation of the fees due will only be made by the authority when they have received the application and checked the submitted documents. Therefore, if the authority disagrees with my calculations you may be required to pay an additional amount. The application will not be considered until the correct fee is received by the authority.

Please let me know if you require any further information.

Yours faithfully

Letter 38

To planning authority, requesting outline approval

Dear Sir

I refer to my discussions with your [*insert name*] with regard to this proposal and I now formally submit an application for outline planning approval on behalf of my client [*insert name*].

I enclose:

1.   Three copies of the form of application duly signed.
2.   Three copies of drawing number [*insert number*] showing the site and its location.
3.   Three copies of drawings numbers [*insert numbers of any other drawings which you wish to include*].
4.   The fee of [*insert amount of fee as appropriate. If no fee is payable, delete this item*].

[Add, if appropriate:]

I hereby certify that the enclosed advertisement has been published on the [*insert dates*] in the [*insert name of local newspaper and add, if appropriate:*] and the said advertisement has been displayed in a prominent position on the site for a period of seven days from [*insert date*].

[*continued*]

Letter 38 continued

If there are any points arising out of this application, I should appreciate a telephone call to resolve them as quickly as possible.

Yours faithfully

Letter 39

To client, if client considering if work should proceed before necessary approvals obtained

Dear Sir

I refer to our recent discussion regarding the progress of this project, when it was suggested that [*insert period*] could be saved by proceeding with the design development without waiting for formal [*insert type*] approval.

I have looked into the matter and the position is that formal approval should be given on [*insert date*]. If all the design work carried out up to that date proves to be abortive, the total professional fees incurred between [*insert date*] and [*insert date*] would be approximately [*insert amount*].

There is, of course, a risk that approval may be refused and some if not all the design development work may be wasted. It is a matter for you to judge in the light of your own particular circumstances which may involve considerations of which I am unaware. If design work is to proceed, there is some urgency to your decision and I will be grateful to receive your written instructions by [*insert date*].

Yours faithfully

Letter 40
To planning authority, requesting renewal of temporary permission

Dear Sir

I refer to temporary planning permission number [*insert number*] granted on the [*insert date*] in respect of the above development. I now formally apply on behalf of my client [*insert name*] for an extension of the duration of the temporary permission until [*insert date*].

[*Add, if appropriate:*]

In support of this application [*state the matters which you consider may influence the authority to extend the duration of the permission*].

If there are any points arising out of this application, I should appreciate a telephone call in order to resolve them as speedily as possible.

Yours faithfully

Copy: Client

Letter 41
To client, seeking information

Dear Sir

Following our meeting on the [*insert date*], I confirm that you
will carry out your own investigations to provide me with the
following information by [*insert date*], so that I can complete my
feasibility studies into this project:

1. The type of ownership of the site/property [*delete as
   appropriate*].
2. Details of restrictive covenants.
3. Details of easements over the site or in connection with
   the site, for example: rights of way, rights of light, rights
   of support, etc.
4. Existing drawings of the site/property [*delete as
   appropriate*].
5. Planning or other approvals already obtained for this
   site/property [*delete as appropriate*].

I anticipate completing my feasibility report by [*insert date*].

Yours faithfully

Letter 42
To client, enclosing the feasibility report

Dear Sir

I enclose [*insert number*] copies of my feasibility report for the
above project. I confirm that I will visit you on the [*insert date*]
at [*insert time*] to discuss the contents and to take your
instructions.

[*If appropriate, add:*]

May I draw your attention particularly to [*insert whatever matter
is most important*].

Yours faithfully

Letter 43
To client, enclosing fee account

Dear Sir

In accordance with the terms of the Standard Form of
Agreement for the Appointment of an Architect 1992, Schedule
Three, I enclose my fee account [*insert number*] which includes
a note of my expenses to [*insert date*].

Prompt payment would be appreciated.

Yours faithfully

Letter 44

To client, if fees are late: first reminder

Dear Sir

I note that my fee account number [*insert number*] of the [*insert date*] is still outstanding.

No doubt the matter has escaped your attention, but I should be pleased if you would let me have your cheque within the next few days. The only way that fees can be kept at a reasonable level in these times of financial stringency is by securing prompt payment.

Yours faithfully

Letter 45
To client, is fees are late: second reminder

Dear Sir

I refer to my fee account number [*insert number*] of the [*insert date*] and my letter of the [*insert date*] in which I requested prompt payment.

I regret that at the time of writing I have not received your cheque and I should be pleased if you would treat this matter with some urgency to avoid unnecessary administrative costs.

Yours faithfully

Letter 46
To client, if fees are late: third reminder

Dear Sir

I refer to my fee account number [*insert number*] of the [*insert date*] which has not yet been paid despite reminders sent to you on the [*insert dates*].

In view of what I always took to be the good working relationship which exists between us, I have not pursued this matter with the vigour it deserves. Although I have no desire to cause problems for you, I must have a care for my own financial position.

May I expect a cheque for the full amount by return of post?

Yours faithfully

Letter 47
To client, if fees are late: legal action threatened

Dear Sir

I refer to my fee account number [*insert number*] of the [*insert date*] in the sum of [*insert amount*].

I have sent you reminders on the [*insert dates*], but I have not yet received payment. I regret, therefore, that if I do not receive your cheque for the full amount by first post on the [*insert date, which should be seven days after the date of this letter*], I shall have no alternative but to instruct my solicitors to commence proceedings for recovery of the debt together with my legal costs.

[*Add, if desired and appropriate:*]

At that time, I will exercise my right to stop all work on this project until I receive full payment.

Yours faithfully

Copy: Solicitor

3 Outline Proposals

Separating the architect's work stages into watertight compartments is recognized as being totally artificial. In reality, your work will tend to flow on and many things will be carried out earlier or later than envisaged by the Plan of Work. Notwithstanding this, the stages form a useful check on progress. During stage C, you will be heavily engaged in producing your basic ideas and there should be little need for letters, standard or otherwise.

Among the matters which may arise is an objection to your outline planning application. Amenity societies keep close watch on all planning applications and you may be faced with what appears to be strong disapproval of your efforts, even before you have come to any firm conclusions about the shape the development will take. Sometimes a polite and co-operative response on your part will deal with the difficulty and you may well find that the amenity society becomes an ally.

This is about the earliest time you can get your client to make firm decisions about the conditions of contract. Very often, he will not be in a position to decide finally until late in stage F. Do not forget that you are expected to have enough legal expertise to advise your client on the form of contract to be used. If he suffers loss, because you have advised him incorrectly, you may be liable.

If the contract to be used is the JCT design and build form (CD 81), it is during this stage that you will be agreeing the contents of the Employer's Requirements with your client.

Letter 48

To client, if amenity society write with objections

Dear Sir

I refer to our telephone conversation of the [*insert date*] when we discussed the objections of the amenity society and I enclose a copy of their letter dated [*insert date*] and my reply dated [*insert date*].

My letter covers the points we discussed and I hope I can allay their fears when I see them.

Yours faithfully

Letter 49
To amenity society, if they write with objections

Dear Sir

Thank you for your letter of the *[insert date]*. I understand and appreciate your reasons for writing. Naturally, I consider this project to satisfy all reasonable requirements in respect of its position in relation to neighbouring buildings and I am confident that it will do more and make a serious contribution to the environment.

However, I am determined to gather as many views as possible, favourable or otherwise, and I suggest that this can best be accomplished if I attend a meeting of your members to listen to them, and to explain the scheme in detail and answer questions.

I will write to you again to arrange a convenient date.

Yours faithfully

Copy: Client

Letter 50a

To client, regarding form of contract to be used
This letter is only suitable for use with JCT 80

Dear Sir

Following our meeting on the [*insert date*] I thought it would
be useful to confirm the decisions reached as follows:

[*Delete as appropriate from the following alternatives:*]

1.   The contract to be used is the JCT Standard Form of
        Building Contract/Local Authorities/Private/With
        Quantities/Without Quantities/With Approximate
        Quantities/1980 with Amendments up to and including
        Amendment 13:1994.
2.   The form will be completed as follows:
        o   Article 3/3A/3B will be used and the words in
                italics struck out/left in.
        o   Article 4: The words in italics will be struck
                out/left in.
        o   The contract will be executed as a deed/by
                sealing/under hand.
        o   Clause 5.3: a master programme is/is not required
                from the contractor/it will be required in network
                analysis or precedence diagram form.
        o   It will be advisable to make provision for clause
                21.2.1 insurance.
        o   Clause 22A/22B/22C is applicable.

[*continued*]

Letter 50a continued

  o Clause 22D insurance may be required.

  o A copy of the appendix is enclosed, completed as agreed.

3. The Sectional Completion Supplement will be used.

4. The Contractor's Designed Portion Supplement will be used.

Please check the contents of this letter carefully and let me know immediately if I have misunderstood your instructions or if there is any point on which you require further clarification.

Yours faithfully

Copy: Quantity surveyor

Letter 50b

To client, regarding form of contract to be used
This letter is only suitable for use with IFC 84

Dear Sir

Following our meeting on the *[insert date]* I thought it would be useful to confirm the decisions reached as follows:

[Delete as appropriate from the following alternatives:]

1.   The contract to be used is the JCT Intermediate Form of Building Contract 1984 with Amendments up to and including Amendment 7:1994.
2.   The form will be completed as follows:
    o   First recital: 'the Architect'/'the Contract Administrator' will be deleted. Delete 'the Specification'/'the Schedules of Work'/'Bills of Quantities'. Delete the final paragraph.
    o   Second recital: delete alternative A/B.
    o   Article 3: delete 'the Architect'/'the Contract Administrator'. The words in italics will be struck out/left in.
    o   Article 4: the words in italics will be struck out/left in.
    o   The contract will be executed as a deed/by sealing/under hand.

[continued]

Letter 50b continued

o   Clause 2.11 from Practice Note IN/1 (revised 1990) will be added.

o   It will be advisable to make provision for clause 6.2.4 insurance.

o   Clause 6.3A/6.3B/6.3C is applicable.

o   Clause 6.3D insurance may be required.

o   A copy of the appendix is enclosed, completed as agreed.

Please check the contents of this letter carefully and let me know immediately if I have misunderstood your instructions or if there is any point on which you require further clarification.

Yours faithfully

Copy: Quantity surveyor

Letter 50c
To client, regarding form of contract to be used
This letter is only suitable for use with MW 80

Dear Sir

Following our meeting on the [*insert date*] I thought it would be useful to confirm the decisions reached as follows:

[*Delete as appropriate from the following alternatives:*]

1.   The contract to be used is the JCT Agreement for Minor Building Works 1980 (1993 revision) with Amendments up to and including Amendment MW8:1994.
2.   The form will be completed as follows:
     o   First recital: 'the Architect'/'the Contract Administrator' will be deleted. Delete 'drawings...Contract Drawings')'/'a Specification...Contract Specification')'/'schedules'.
     o   Second recital: delete 'the Specification'/'or the schedules'/'or provided a schedule of rates'.
     o   Fourth recital: delete.
     o   Article 3: 'the Architect'/'the Contract Administrator' will be deleted.
     o   Article 4: delete 'Royal Institute of British Architects'/'Royal Institution of Chartered Surveyors'.

[*continued*]

Letter 50c continued

o   The contract will be executed as a deed/by
         sealing/under hand.

o   Clause 2.1: the date for commencement will be
         [*insert date*] and the date for completion will be
         [*insert date*].

o   Clause 2.3: the liquidated damages will be [*insert
         amount*] per [*insert 'day' or 'week'*].

o   Clause 2.5: the defects liability period will be
         [*insert period*].

o   Clauses 3.6 and 4.1: deletions as appropriate to
         follow recitals.

o   Clauses 4.2 and 4.3: the retention percentage will
         be [*insert percentage*].

o   Clause 4.4: the period will be [*insert period*].

o   Clause 4.5 will/will not be deleted.

o   Clause 5.2 will be completed when the contractor
         is known.

o   Clause 6.3A will apply and the percentage to cover
         professional fees will be [*insert percentage*].

o   Clause 6.3B will apply.

o   Clause 9.5 is/is not to apply.

[*continued*]

Letter 50c continued

Please check the contents of this letter carefully and let me know immediately if I have misunderstood your instructions or if there is any point on which you require further clarification.

Yours faithfully

Copy: Quantity surveyor [*if appointed*]

Letter 51

To client, regarding the content of the Employer's Requirements
This letter is only suitable for use with CD 81

Dear Sir

It is part of my duty to prepare the Employer's Requirements which will form part of the contract. It is an important document, because it is what the Contractor's Proposals must satisfy. Therefore, it must include all relevant matters. It is essential that we spend some time discussing the content and I believe that the best way to ensure maximum use of time is to have an agenda. Perhaps you would give the following items some thought before we meet. I will telephone you within the next few days after you have had the opportunity to digest the contents of this letter:

[List the matters which require consideration. They may include some or all of the following:

o Details of site and boundaries.
o Details of accommodation requirements.
o Purposes for which the building is to be used.
o Any other matter likely to affect the preparation of the Contractor's Proposals and his price.

[continued]

Letter 51 continued

o *Statement of functional and ancillary requirements:*
     - kind and number of buildings
     - density and mix of dwellings
     - height limitations
     - specific requirements for finishes
o *Provisional sums.*
o *Planning constraints.*
o *Restrictive or other covenants.*
o *Statutory or other permissions.*
o *Site requirements.*
o *The mandatory extent of the Employer's Requirements.*
o *Access restrictions.*
o *Availability of public utilities.*
o *Presentation of Contractor's Proposals.*
o *Submission of contractor's drawings.*
o *Detailed as-built drawings requirements.*
o *Stage or periodic payments.*
o *Functions of the employer's agent.*
o *Information required to complete the contract appendices.*]

Yours faithfully

Copy: Quantity surveyor [*if appointed*]

Letter 52

To client, regarding form of contract to be used
This letter is only suitable for use with CD 81

Dear Sir

Following our meeting on the [*insert date*] I thought it would
be useful to confirm the decisions reached as follows:

[*Delete as appropriate from the following alternatives:*]

1. The contract to be used is the JCT Standard Form of
    Building Contract With Contractor's Design 1981 with
    Amendments up to and including Amendment 7:1994.
2. The form will be completed as follows:
    o   The contract will be executed as a deed/by
        sealing/under hand.
    o   It will be advisable to make provision for clause
        21.2.1 insurance.
    o   Clause 22A/22B/22C insurance is applicable.
    o   Clause 22D insurance may be required.
    o   Clause 30.4.2.2 will be deleted and a replacement
        clause will be drafted to express the intentions of
        the parties not to place the retention in a separate
        banking account.
    o   Clause 30.5.3.11 will be deleted.
    o   Supplementary provisions S1/S2/S3/S4/S5/S6/S7
        will apply.

[*continued*]

Letter 52 continued

3.   The sectional completion modifications will apply.
4.   A copy of appendices 1, 2 and 3 are enclosed, completed
     as agreed.

Please check the contents of this letter carefully and let me
know immediately if I have misunderstood your instructions or if
there is any point on which you require further clarification.

Yours faithfully

Copy: Quantity surveyor [*if appointed*]

Letter 53

To client, enclosing outline proposals report

Dear Sir

I have completed my outline proposals for this project and I
have pleasure in enclosing [*insert number*] copies of my report
and drawings numbers [*insert numbers*] illustrating the scheme.

I confirm that I will visit you on the [*insert date*] at [*insert
time*] to discuss my report and to receive your instructions.

[*If appropriate, add:*]

Will you give special consideration to [*insert as appropriate*].

Yours faithfully

4 Scheme Design

During this stage you will be finalizing your design and ironing out any problems with the relevant authorities. At the end of this stage, you may think it wise to prepare a brief report to submit to your client with your presentation drawings, but you must make clear that changes in requirements after this point will delay the project and result in extra fees.

Letter 54

To manufacturer, asking for technical literature

Dear Sir

I should be pleased to receive full technical details of [*insert name of product*].

Please note that I do not wish to meet your representative at this stage. If your literature indicates that your product is appropriate to my requirements, I may request further assistance in due course.

Yours faithfully

Letter 55
To manufacturer, asking representative to visit for general purposes

Dear Sir

I am interested in [*insert name of product*] and I should be
pleased if you would ask your technical representative to
telephone to make an appointment to see me within [*insert time
period*].

Please note that he must be prepared to supply details of
projects on which your product has been used successfully and
fact sheets for my office library.

Yours faithfully

Letter 56
To manufacturer, asking representative to visit for special purposes

Dear Sir

I am considering the use of [*insert name of product*] on a new project and I require some technical advice.

Please arrange for your technical representative to telephone to make an appointment to visit me at this office/meet on site [*delete as appropriate*]. He should be prepared to supply precise and substantiated facts and a list of projects where [*insert name of product*] has been used successfully.

Yours faithfully

Letter 57
To manufacturer, asking for letter

Dear Sir

Following our meeting on the [*insert date*] to discuss the use of [*insert name of product*] on this project, I am prepared to specify its use if you will write to me unequivocally confirming that [*insert name of product*] will satisfy my client's requirements. I confirm that we discussed those requirements in detail, but they may be summarised non-exclusively as [*summarise the client's requirements in respect of the product, clearly and concisely*].

I look forward to receiving your letter by [*insert date*] at latest.

Yours faithfully

Letter 58

To local authority environmental services department, enclosing sketch plans

---

Dear Sir

I act as architect for the above development. My client is
[*insert name*].

I enclose two copies of each of drawings numbers [*insert
numbers*] showing sketch plans and layout of the proposals and I
should be grateful if you would examine the proposals and let
me have your acceptance or comments on the refuse collection
arrangements indicated.

Yours faithfully

Letter 59
To fire prevention officer, enclosing sketch plans

Dear Sir

I act as architect for the above development. My client is
[*insert name*].

I enclose two copies of each of drawings numbers [*insert
numbers*] showing sketch plans, elevations and sections of the
proposal and I should be grateful if you would examine the
proposals and let me have your recommendations and
observations.

[*You may wish to add:*]

After studying your comments, I will telephone to arrange a
meeting with other members of the design team to iron out any
difficulties.

Yours faithfully

Letter 60
To British Telecom, enclosing sketch layout

Dear Sir

I refer to previous correspondence of the [*insert dates of all previous letters to and from British Telecom*]. I enclose two copies of my preliminary layout of the site including the inlet positions of all telephone services/the telephone service [*delete as appropriate*] coloured green. This is drawing number [*insert number*].

[*Add, if appropriate:*]

The cable to be diverted is shown coloured red.

[*Then:*]

A temporary service will be required on site for the duration of the project. It will be paid for by the main contractor who will send his order when appointed. The relevant programme dates are as follows:

Commencement of project: [*insert date*].
Completion of project: [*insert date*].
Telephone service required: [*insert date*].
Diversion to be completed: [*insert date if appropriate*].

[*continued*]

Letter 60 continued

I should be pleased if you would return one copy of the plan showing the service line[s] and any other provision required [*if cable is to be diverted, add:*] including your firm price quotation for carrying out the diversion of the cable coloured red and making good.

Yours faithfully

Letter 61
To electricity supplier, enclosing sketch layout

Dear Sir

I refer to previous correspondence of the [*insert dates of all previous letters to and from the electricity supplier*]. I enclose two copies of my preliminary layout of the site including the inlet positions of all electrical services/the electricity service [*delete as appropriate*] coloured green. This is drawing number [*insert number*].

[*Add, if appropriate:*]

The main to be diverted is shown coloured red.

[*Then:*]

The service[s] required is/are [*delete as appropriate then insert details*]. The relevant programme dates are anticipated to be as follows:

Commencement of project: [*insert date*].
Completion of project: [*insert date*].
Electricity service required: [*insert date*].
Diversion to be completed: [*insert date if appropriate*].

[*continued*]

Letter 61 continued

I should be pleased if you would return one copy of the plan showing the service line[s] and any other provision required together with your firm price quotation for carrying out the work [*if main is to be diverted, add:*] including diversion of the main and all necessary making good.

Yours faithfully

Letter 62
To gas supplier, enclosing sketch layout

Dear Sir

I refer to previous correspondence of the [*insert dates of all previous letters to and from the gas supplier*]. I enclose two copies of my preliminary layout of the site including the inlet positions of all gas services/the gas service [*delete as appropriate*] coloured green. This is drawing number [*insert number*].

[*Add, if appropriate:*]

The main to be diverted is shown coloured red.

[*Then:*]

The relevant programme dates are anticipated to be as follows:

Commencement of project: [*insert date*].
Completion of project: [*insert date*].
Gas service required: [*insert date*].
Diversion to be completed: [*insert date if appropriate*].

[*continued*]

Letter 62 continued

I should be pleased if you would return one copy of the plan showing the service line[s] together with your firm price quotation for carrying out the work [*if main is to be diverted, add:*] including diversion of the main and all necessary making good.

Yours faithfully

Letter 63
To water supplier, enclosing sketch layout

Dear Sir

I refer to previous correspondence of the [*insert dates of all previous letters to and from the water supplier*]. I enclose two copies of my preliminary layout of the site including the inlet positions of all water services/the water service [*delete as appropriate*] coloured green. This is drawing number [*insert number*].

[*Add, if appropriate:*]

The main to be diverted is shown coloured red.

[*Then:*]

The relevant programme dates are anticipated to be as follows:

Commencement of project: [*insert date*].
Completion of project: [*insert date*].
Water service required: [*insert date*].
Diversion to be completed: [*insert date if appropriate*].

[*continued*]

Letter 63 continued

I should be pleased if you would return one copy of the plan showing the service line[s] together with your firm price quotation for carrying out the work [*if main is to be diverted, add:*] including diversion of the main and all necessary making good.

Yours faithfully

Letter 64
To highway authority, enclosing sketch layout

Dear Sir

I refer to previous correspondence of the [*insert dates of all previous letters to and from the highway authority*]. I enclose two copies of my preliminary layout of the site including all proposed roads, footpaths and means of ingress and egress. This is drawing number [*insert number*].

I should be pleased to receive your approval or comments in detail so that I can make progress in completing my design. In particular, may I have your observations on the following:

[*Delete as appropriate from the following:*]

1. Road and footpath widths.
2. Sight lines.
3. Diversion of existing highway.
4. Stopping of existing highway.
5. Street lighting.
6. Procedure for obtaining formal consent from your authority to the enclosed proposals.
7. Procedure for obtaining consent to the adoption of the roads and footpaths coloured green.

Yours faithfully

Letter 65

To environmental health authority, regarding Clean Air Acts

Dear Sir

I understand that the above development may be subject to special design requirements under the Clean Air Acts.

I enclose two copies of each of my drawings numbers [*insert numbers*] and I should be pleased to receive your comments.

Since design development is continuing, I will telephone you during the next few days in order to obtain your initial reactions to the scheme.

Yours faithfully

Letter 66

To client, enclosing the scheme design report

Dear Sir

I have pleasure in enclosing my scheme design report and drawings numbers *[insert numbers]* showing my detailed proposals for this project.

I confirm that I will meet you on *[insert date]* at *[insert time]* at *[insert place]* and I look forward to discussing matters arising from my report and taking your instructions for the next stage.

[If appropriate, add:]

I should be grateful if you would carefully consider *[insert as appropriate]* before our meeting.

Yours faithfully

Letter 67
To client, regarding modification of the brief

Dear Sir

I confirm your approval of the scheme design shown on my
drawing number [*insert drawing number*] subject to the
following modifications:

[*Briefly describe the modifications*]

I am now completing the detailed design with all speed. Any
modifications to the brief after this point would have serious
effect on the time schedule for the project and, since redesigning
would be necessary, extra fees would be chargeable.

Yours faithfully

5   Detail Design

Drawing board rather than desk during this stage, but you must stress that, at the end, the proposals can only be altered at considerable expense.

Letter 68
To client, regarding modifications to size, shape, location or cost

Dear Sir

I confirm that the detailed design work for the above project is now complete and I have commenced preparing the production information necessary for construction.

I know that you appreciate the problems caused by changes of mind at this stage. Any further alterations to the size, shape, location or cost of the project will make much of the completed work abortive which, in turn, will involve delays and additional fees.

Yours faithfully

Letter 69

To client, regarding promptness of decisions

Dear Sir

This is perhaps an opportune moment to ask you to review your arrangements for providing urgent decisions.

I am sure you appreciate that there will be certain points during the currency of the contract which must be referred to you; although I am always ready to give you my professional advice where appropriate.

In such circumstances, it is essential to obtain a quick decision in the interests of avoiding delays and extra costs.

If it is possible for you to nominate one person with full powers to make any urgent decisions that would be entirely satisfactory.

Yours faithfully

6 Production Information

Most architects would agree that this is the busiest stage; the constructional drawings and schedules must be prepared, outstanding approvals obtained and arrangements put in hand for tendering for sub-contract, for supply and for main contract work. Where CD 81 is being used, you will be busily engaged in putting together the Employer's Requirements. Since it is essentially a performance specification, its composition is no mean task.

Fortunately, a good many of the administrative letters can be standard. It has been assumed that you will be applying for approval under the Building Regulations in the usual way. This would appear to be the pattern in the future. If you intend to deal with the Building Regulations under one of the possible alternatives, you must produce your own letter to suit.

Tendering can be a long process if measured from the collection of names for the tender list. To start as early as possible is the answer. All architects have their own lists of contractors who have done good work in the past, but you must check with the client. Never simply accept a name from him; carry out your own checks and do not hesitate to tell your client if you are doubtful about the financial standing or capability of a firm which he asks to be included. Never recommend a contractor to your client; it is not your place to do so and it is very dangerous, because you cannot know whether changes in a company's personnel or their financial situation will cause them to produce a vastly different result from what you have come to expect from them.

Letter 70
To client, requesting fees for Building Regulations application

Dear Sir

I anticipate being in a position to make application for Building Regulation approval on the [*insert date*]. The local authority is required to charge fees in accordance with a schedule of charges. The application will not be considered until the correct fee is received by the authority.

I have calculated the fee payable in respect of this application as [*insert amount*] and I should be pleased to receive your cheque for this amount which you should draw in favour of [*insert name of authority*]. Please note that after the authority have carried out their first inspection on site, a further fee will become payable in accordance with the scale.

Please let me know if you require further information.

Yours faithfully

Letter 71

To client, requesting fees for Planning and Building Regulations application

Dear Sir

I anticipate being in a position to make application for full planning permission and approval under the Building Regulations on the [*insert date*]. A separate fee is payable in respect of each application. Until the fee is received by the authority, the application will not be considered.

I have calculated the fees payable as follows:

Planning application: [*insert amount*].
Building Regulations application: [*insert amount*].

I should be pleased if you would draw a single cheque in the sum of [*insert total amount*] in favour of [*insert name of authority*]. If you will send the cheque to me, I will attach it to the application. Please note that after the authority have carried out their first inspection on site under the Building Regulations, a further fee will become payable in accordance with the scale.

Please let me know if you require any further information.

Yours faithfully

Letter 72
To planning authority, requesting approval of reserved matters

Dear Sir

I refer to outline planning permission number [*insert number*] granted on the [*insert date*] in respect of the above development. I now formally apply on behalf of my client [*insert name*] for approval of the following reserved matters:

[*List the reserved matters exactly as they appear on the original permission. If approval is sought for certain matters only, list only those matters*].

In support of this application, I enclose three copies of drawings numbers [*insert numbers*].

If there is likely to be any difficulty in obtaining approval, I should appreciate a telephone call so that such difficulties can be resolved as soon as possible.

Yours faithfully

Copy: Client

Letter 73

To planning authority, applying for full planning approval

Dear Sir

I refer to my discussions with your [*insert name*] with regard to this proposal and outline planning permission dated [*insert date*]. I now formally submit an application for full planning permission on behalf of my client [*insert name*].

I enclose:

1.   Three copies of the completed form of application.
2.   Three copies of drawings numbers [*insert numbers*].
3.   The fee of [*insert amount of fee as appropriate. If no fee is payable, delete this item*].
4.   Certificate A/B/C/D [*delete as appropriate*].

[*Add, if appropriate:*]

I hereby certify that the enclosed advertisement has been published on the [*insert dates*] in the [*insert name of local newspaper and add, if appropriate:*] and the said advertisement has been displayed in a prominent position on the site for a period of seven days from [*insert date*].

[*continued*]

Letter 73 continued

If there are any matters which could prevent or delay the granting of full planning permission, I should appreciate a telephone call so that such matters can be resolved as quickly as possible.

Yours faithfully

Letter 74

To planning authority, applying for full planning permission and Building Regulations approval

Dear Sir

I refer to my discussions with [*insert name*] in your planning department and [*insert name*] in building control. Outline planning permission number [*insert number*] was granted on [*insert date*]. I now formally submit an application for full planning permission and approval under the Building Regulations on behalf of my client [*insert name*].

I enclose:

1.   Five copies of the completed form of application.
2.   Five copies of drawings numbers [*insert numbers*].
3.   The fee of [*insert amount of fee as appropriate. If no fee is payable, delete this item*].
4.   Certificate A/B/C/D [*delete as appropriate*].

[*Add, if appropriate:*]

I hereby certify that the enclosed advertisement has been published on the [*insert dates*] in the [*insert name of local newspaper and add, if appropriate:*] and the said advertisement has been displayed in a prominent position on the site for a period of seven days from [*insert date*].

[*continued*]

Letter 74 continued

Formal consultations have been carried out with HM Factory Inspectorate (Health and Safety Executive) and the appropriate certificate is enclosed.

If there are any matters which could prevent or delay granting of planning permission or approval under the Building Regulations, I should be grateful if you would telephone me immediately so that such matters can be resolved without delay.

Yours faithfully

Copy: Client

Letter 75
To local authority, requesting Building Regulations Approval

Dear Sir

I refer to my discussions with [*insert name*] in your building control department. I now formally submit an application for approval under the Building Regulations on behalf of my client [*insert name*].

I enclose:

1.   Two copies of the completed form of application.
2.   Two copies of drawings numbers [*insert numbers*].
3.   The fee of [*insert amount of fee as appropriate. If no fee is payable, delete this item*].

[*Add, if appropriate:*]

I have commenced/completed [*delete as appropriate*] formal consultations with HM Inspectorate (Health and Safety Executive) and a fire certificate is enclosed/will be forwarded in the near future [*delete as appropriate*].

I should appreciate a telephone call if any point arises which might prevent or delay approval.

Yours faithfully

Letter 76
To HM Inspectorate (Health and Safety Executive), applying for fire certificate

Dear Sir

I understand that the above development is of a nature that requires me to carry out formal consultations with HM Inspectorate in order to obtain a fire certificate under the Fire Certificate (Special Premises) Regulations 1976.

I enclose two copies of each of drawings numbers [*insert numbers*] showing details of my proposals which I hereby submit on behalf of my client [*insert name*].

Applications for approval under the Building Regulations is being submitted to [*insert name of authority*] at [*insert address*] during the course of the next few days and I should appreciate it if you would inform me if you require any further information.

Yours faithfully

Copy: Client

Letter 77
To client, regarding main contractor tender list

Dear Sir

In accordance with the agreed timetable for this project, I shall be inviting tenders on your behalf on or about the [*insert date*] using the Code of Procedure for Single Stage Selective Tendering 1994.

I will discuss the tendering procedure with you in more detail, but at this stage I should be pleased to know if you wish to nominate any contractors for inclusion on the tender list. I already have several contractors in mind who could be suitable, and when I have completed the necessary enquiries I will meet you to draw up the final list.

Yours faithfully

Letter 78

To client, regarding main contractor tender list if two stage tendering is to be used

Dear Sir

In accordance with the agreed timetable for this project, I shall be inviting tenders on your behalf on or about the [*insert date*] using the Code of Procedure for Two Stage Selective Tendering 1994 as discussed at our recent meeting.

I should be pleased to know if you wish to nominate any contractors for inclusion on the tender list. I already have several contractors in mind who could be suitable, and when I have completed the necessary enquiries I will meet you to draw up the final list.

Yours faithfully

Letter 79
To client, confirming tender details

Dear Sir

Following our discussions on the [*insert date*], I thought it would be useful to confirm the decisions you made with regard to the invitation of tenders as follows:

1.   Contractors to be invited to tender: [*list*].
2.   Period of time allowed for tendering: [*insert period*].
3.   Date, time and place for receipt of tenders: [*insert details*].
4.   Tender to remain open for acceptance for: [*insert period*].
5.   Alternative 1/2 [*delete as appropriate*] of the Code of Procedure for Single Stage Selective Tendering 1994 to apply.

Yours faithfully

Letter 80

To donor, returning gift

Dear Sir

Thank you for your gift which I received today.

I am sure that you understand that I cannot allow anything to throw the slightest doubt upon my professional integrity. For this reason I am following my usual policy and returning the gift to you.

That is not to say, however, that I do not appreciate the thought which prompted your action.

Yours faithfully

Letter 81
To prospective nominated or named sub-contractor/person, enquiring if willing to submit a tender

Dear Sir

I have been instructed by my client, [*insert name*], to prepare a list of firms willing to tender for [*insert nature of work*] on the above project. Please inform me in writing, not later than [*insert date*] if you wish to be included. If you are unable to tender on this occasion, it will not prejudice your inclusion on tender lists for other projects under my direction, but you should note that your agreement to tender does not guarantee that you will receive an invitation to do so. The following is set out for your information: [*Insert information appropriate to your project in the following items*]

1. Name of project:
2. Name of employer:
3. Name of architect:
4. Name of quantity surveyor:
5. Name of consultants:
6. Site address:
7. General description of work:
8. Approximate cost range:
9. Form of main contract to be used:
10. Contract clauses to be deleted:

[*continued*]

Letter 81 continued

---

11. Special additional clauses:
12. Form of sub-contract to be used:
13. Contract clauses to be deleted:
14. Special additional clauses:
15. The contract is to be executed under hand/as a deed [*delete as appropriate*].
16. Anticipated date for possession in main contract:
17. Period for completion of the main contract works:
18. Approximate date for despatch of tender documents:
19. Tender period:
20. Tender to remain open for acceptance for [*insert figure*] weeks.
21. Liquidated damages in main contract:

Yours faithfully

Letter 82
To prospective contractor, enclosing questionnaire

Dear Sir

I anticipate inviting tenders for the above project on or about
[*insert date*]. The works will consist of [*insert brief description*].
If you wish to be considered for inclusion on the list of
contractors invited to tender, please let me have the following
information by [*insert date*]:

1.　　Names and addresses of all directors.
2.　　Address of your registered office.
3.　　Share capital of the firm.
4.　　Annual turnover during the last three years.
5.　　Number and positions of all office-based staff.
6.　　Number of site operatives permanently employed in each
　　　trade.
7.　　Number of trained supervisory staff permanently on site.
8.　　Number and value of current contracts on site.
9.　　Address, date of completion and value of three projects
　　　of similar character to that for which tenders are to be
　　　invited and which have been carried out by your firm
　　　recently.
10.　　Names and addresses of clients, architects and quantity
　　　surveyors connected with the projects noted in 9 above
　　　and to whom reference may be made.

Yours faithfully

Letter 83

To referee, regarding suitability of contractor

Dear Sir

[*Insert name of contractor*] have informed me that they have
recently completed a project for you. I am considering including
them in the list of tenderers to carry out the above work which
will consist of [*insert brief description of the work*].

I should be grateful if you would complete the following
questions and return them to me in the enclosed stamped
addressed envelope. Your answers and any other comments you
care to make will remain strictly confidential.

1.   Would you use this firm again?
2.   How would you describe the quality of workmanship
      relative to the quality specified?
3.   Was site supervision satisfactory?
4.   Was head office organisation satisfactory?
5.   Were staff helpful and efficient?
6.   Were relations good between the contractor, sub-
      contractors, nominated sub-contractors, suppliers and
      employer's licensees?
7.   So far as you are aware, did the contractor pay his sub-
      contractors and suppliers promptly and in full?

[*continued*]

Letter 83 continued

8. Does this firm normally complete on time in your experience?

9. Do you consider their attitude to claims fair and reasonable?

Yours faithfully

Letter 84
To contractor, enquiring if contractor is willing to submit a tender

Dear Sir

I have been instructed by my client, [*insert name*], to prepare a list of firms willing to tender for the above project. Please inform me in writing, not later than [*insert date*], if you wish to be included. If you are unable to tender on this occasion, it will not prejudice your inclusion on tender lists for other projects under my direction, but you should note that your agreement to tender does not guarantee that you will receive an invitation to do so.

The tendering procedure will be in accordance with the Code of Procedure for Single Stage Selective Tendering 1994 and all firms wishing to be included on the tender list will be deemed to have fully informed themselves of its contents. The following is set out for your information:
[*Insert information appropriate to your project in the following items:*]

1. Name of project:
2. Name of employer:
3. Name of architect:
4. Name of quantity surveyor:

[*continued*]

Letter 84 continued

5.   Name of consultants:

6.   Site address:

7.   General description of work:

8.   Approximate cost range:

9.   Items for which it is anticipated that nominated sub-contractors will be used:

10.   Form of contract to be used:

11.   Contract clauses to be deleted:

12.   Special additional clauses:

13.   Examination and correction of priced bills: Alternative 1/Alternative 2 [*delete as appropriate*] will apply.

14.   The contract is to be executed under hand/as a deed [*delete as appropriate*].

15.   Anticipated date for possession:

16.   Period for completion of the works:

17.   Approximate date for despatch of tender documents:

18.   Tender period:

19.   Tender to remain open for acceptance for [*insert figure*] weeks.

20.   Liquidated damages:

21.   Bond required:

Yours faithfully

Letter 85
To unsuccessful sub-contractors and suppliers

Dear Sir

Your tender for [*insert description of work or goods*] was not successful.

Tenders received were as follows:

[*List amounts in ascending order. Names of tenderers may also be listed, separately in alphabetical order unless to do so would make it possible to link tenderers with amounts*].

You may be assured that I will be happy to approach you again on future occasions.

Yours faithfully

Letter 86
To client, regarding letter of intent to sub-contractors and suppliers

Dear Sir

In response to your instructions received on the [*insert date*], I enclose a draft letter of intent which I propose to send to the following sub-contractors/suppliers [*delete as appropriate*]:

[*List firms and immediate work or goods required*]

I should be pleased to receive your agreement as soon as possible.

Yours faithfully

Letter 87
To sub-contractor or supplier: letter of intent

Dear Sir

My client, [*insert name*], has instructed me to inform you that
your tender of the [*insert date*] in the sum of [*insert amount*]
for [*insert the nature of the work or goods*] is acceptable and
that I intend to instruct the main contractor to enter into a sub-
contract/place an order [*delete as appropriate*] after the main
contract has been signed.

It is not my client's intention that this letter should be evidence
of a binding contract. However, my client is prepared to instruct
you to [*insert details of the limited nature of the work or goods
required*]. If, for any reason whatsoever, no contract is entered
into with you for this work/these goods [*delete as appropriate*],
my client's commitment will be strictly limited to payment,
through the main contractor, for [*insert the limited nature of the
work or goods required*].

No other work/goods [*delete as appropriate*] included in your
tender must be carried out/supplied [*delete as appropriate*]
without a further written order. No further obligation is placed
upon my client and no obligation whatsoever, under any
circumstances, is placed upon me.

Yours faithfully

Letter 88

To client, confirming the amount of liquidated damages

Dear Sir

Following our meeting of the [*insert date*], I confirm that the figure which you have agreed as liquidated and ascertained damages to be inserted in the contract documents is £ [*insert amount*] per week. The figure is calculated as follows:

[*List and total the weekly sums taken into account*].

Yours faithfully

Copy: Quantity surveyor

7 Bills of Quantities

Few standard letters during this stage. You will be clearing up items outstanding from the last stage, answering questions from the quantity surveyor and probably completing some drawings.

You must decide whether to recommend the appointment of a clerk of works so that the appropriate provision can be made in the bills of quantities. Some clients offer initial resistance to the idea of a clerk of works, presumably because they object to paying additional money to someone to carry out what they see as being your function. You must be firm.

This may be the time when you realise that despatch of tenders will be delayed. As soon as you have some idea of the length of the delay, notify the tenderers. It is not only courteous, it makes good sense to keep them informed. Otherwise you may suffer the embarrassment, to say the least, of having some of your documents returned.

Letter 89
To client, if clerk of works required

Dear Sir

This appears to be a suitable time to consider the appointment of a clerk of works for this project. The duty of a clerk of works is to act as an inspector of the works on your behalf and under my direction.

It is my view that the size/complexity/nature [*delete as appropriate*] of the work demands constant/frequent [*delete as appropriate*] inspections and I recommend the employment of a clerk of works in a full-time/part-time [*delete as appropriate*] basis in accordance with clause 3.3.1 of the RIBA Standard Form of Agreement for the Appointment of an Architect.

It is normal practice for you to appoint the clerk of works directly, but I shall be happy to advise you about the administrative details involved. Perhaps you will telephone when you have had a chance to consider the matter.

Yours faithfully

Letter 90
To all contractors on tender list, if date delayed

Dear Sir

I refer to your letter of the [*insert date*] indicating your willingness to submit a tender for the above project.

Unforeseen circumstances have obliged me to reassess the date for despatch of tender documents. The date for despatch is now expected to be [*insert date*].

I should be grateful if you would check your programme and confirm, by return if possible, that you are still willing to submit a tender.

Yours faithfully

8   Tender Action

It is recommended that you follow the procedure laid down in the Code of Procedure for Single Stage Selective Tendering 1989 (Alternatives are the Code of Procedure for Two Stage Selective Tendering 1983 and the Code of Procedure for Selective Tendering for Design and Build 1985). The standard letters have been composed on that basis. Keep your client informed. Usually, he will wish to be present when tenders are opened. If not, it is good practice to open them in the presence of a witness.

Letter 91

To contractor, inviting him to tender if bills of quantities included

Dear Sir

I refer you to your letter of the *[insert date]* in which you expressed a willingness to submit a tender for the above project. I now have pleasure in enclosing the following:

1.   Two copies of the bills of quantities.
2.   Two copies of each of drawings numbers *[insert numbers]* giving a general indication of the scope and character of the works.
      These will become the contract drawings.
3.   Two copies of the form of tender.
4.   An addressed envelope for the return of the tender and instructions relating thereto.

Please note the following:

a.   A full set of drawings may be inspected at *[insert place]*.
b.   The site may be inspected by arrangement with *[insert the person and telephone number]*.
c.   Tendering will be in accordance with the Code of Procedure for Single Stage Selective Tendering 1994.
d.   Examination and adjustment of priced bills - Alternative 1/Alternative 2 *[delete as appropriate]* of clause 6 of the Code will apply.

[continued]

Letter 91 continued

The completed form of tender is to be sealed in the endorsed envelope provided and must arrive at [*insert place*] not later than [*insert time*] on [*insert date*].

Please acknowledge safe receipt of this letter together with the enclosures noted and confirm that you will submit a tender in accordance with these instructions.

Yours faithfully

Copies: Employer
Quantity surveyor

Letter 92

To contractor, inviting him to tender if bills of quantities not included

Dear Sir

I refer to your letter of the [*insert date*] in which you expressed willingness to submit a tender for the above project. I now have pleasure in enclosing the following:

1. Two copies of the specification/schedule of rates/schedule of activities/schedule of work [*delete as appropriate*].
2. Two copies of each of drawings numbers [*insert numbers*]. These will become the contract drawings.
3. Two copies of the form of tender.
4. An addressed envelope for the return of the tender and instructions relating thereto.

Please note the following:

a. The site may be inspected by arrangement with [*insert the person and telephone number*].
b. Tendering will be in accordance with the Code of Procedure for Single Stage Selective Tendering 1994.

[continued]

Letter 92 continued

The completed form of tender is to be sealed in the endorsed envelope provided and must arrive at [*insert place*] not later than [*insert time*] on [*insert date*].

Please acknowledge safe receipt of this letter together with the enclosures noted and confirm that you will submit a tender in accordance with these instructions.

Yours faithfully

Copies: Employer
Quantity surveyor

Letter 93
To client and quantity surveyor, enclosing copy of invitation to tender

Dear Sir

I have today sent tender documents to all the contractors on the agreed list of tenderers for the above project. A copy of my covering letter is enclosed for your information.

Yours faithfully

Letter 94
To all contractors, regarding questions during the tender period

Dear Sir

I refer to the invitation to tender sent to you on [*insert date*] in respect of the above project.

The following is a list of all the questions which have been asked and the replies given at today's date:

[*List questions and answers clearly and concisely*]

The above information and clarification is to be taken as part of, and will override, the tender documentation as indicated.

[*Add, if appropriate:*]

Please note that the date for receipt of tenders has been changed to [*insert new date*] to take account of the above amendments. The time and place for receipt of tenders remains unchanged.

Yours faithfully

Letter 95
To client, regarding opening of tenders

Dear Sir

I refer to our recent telephone conversation and confirm that main contract tenders should be received at this office on [*insert date*]. The deadline for receipt of tenders is [*insert time*].

Tenders will be opened at [*insert time*] after you arrive. I have spoken to [*insert name*], the quantity surveyor, who has arranged to be present to assist in assessing the tenders.

I look forward to seeing you.

Yours faithfully

Letter 96
To contractor who submits a qualified tender

Dear Sir

Tenders for the above project were opened on [*insert date*] and it was noted that you had submitted a qualified tender.

The invitation to tender sent to you on the [*insert date*] stated that tendering was to be in accordance with the Code of Procedure for Single Stage Selective Tendering 1994 which prohibits qualified tenders by clause 4.4.

If you wish your tender to be considered, please inform me in writing by [*insert date*] that you withdraw the qualification without amendment to your tender. Failure to so notify me will result in your tender being rejected.

Yours faithfully

Letter 97
To contractors who submit the second and third lowest tenders

Dear Sir

Tenders for the above project were opened on the [*insert date*] and I have to inform you that your tender was second/third [*delete as appropriate*] lowest.

Although not the most favourable, it may be that your tender will be given further consideration, in which case I will notify you again. I will, of course, notify you immediately if a decision is taken to accept another tender.

Yours faithfully

Copies: Employer
        Quantity surveyor

Letter 98
To contractors not among the three lowest tenderers

Dear Sir

Tenders for the above project were opened on the [*insert date*] and I have to inform you that your price was not among the lowest three submitted.

Although you were not successful in this instance, you can be sure that it will not adversely affect future enquiries from this office.

A full list of all the prices submitted will be sent to you in due course.

Yours faithfully

Letter 99
To contractors who submit the second and third lowest tenders if another tender accepted

Dear Sir

I refer to my letter of the [*insert date*].

My client has decided to accept another tender. I thank you for being prepared to stand by your tender and, although you were not successful in this instance, you can be sure that it will not adversely affect future enquiries from this office.

A full list of all the prices submitted will be sent to you in due course.

Yours faithfully

Copies: Employer
         Quantity surveyor

Letter 100
To contractor who submits the lowest tender, but with errors to be dealt with under Alternative 1

Dear Sir

The quantity surveyor has now completed his examination of your priced bills in connection with the above project and he has detected the following errors:

[*List errors by page and item number*]

In accordance with Alternative 1 of clause 6 of the Code of Procedure for Single Stage Selective Tendering 1994, you may now send me written notice confirming or withdrawing your offer.

If you confirm your offer, an endorsement will be added to the priced bills indicating that all rates or prices (excluding preliminary items, contingencies, prime cost and provisional sums) inserted therein are to be considered as reduced/increased [*delete as appropriate*] in the same proportion as the corrected total of priced items falls short of/exceeds [*delete as appropriate*] such items.

Yours faithfully

Copies: Employer
          Quantity surveyor

Letter 101

To contractor who submits lowest tender, but with errors to be dealt with under Alternative 2

Dear Sir

The quantity surveyor has now completed his examination of your priced bills in connection with the above project and he has detected the following errors:

[*List errors by page and item number*]

In accordance with Alternative 2 of clause 6 of the Code of Procedure for Single Stage Selective Tendering 1994, you may now confirm your offer or amend it to correct the errors.

If you confirm your offer, an endorsement will be added to the priced bills indicating that all rates or prices (excluding preliminary items, contingencies, prime cost and provisional sums) inserted therein are to be considered as reduced/increased [*delete as appropriate*] in the same proportion as the corrected total of priced items falls short of/exceeds [*delete as appropriate*] such items. If you amend your offer and it is no longer lowest, the lowest tender will be considered.

Yours faithfully

Copies: Employer
Quantity surveyor

Letter 102
To contractor, accepting tender
Registered Post/Recorded Delivery

Dear Sir

My client [*insert name*] has instructed me to inform you that he
accepts your tender dated [*insert date*] in the sum of [*insert
amount in words*] for the above work in accordance with
drawings numbers [*insert numbers*] and the bills of quantities
[*or specification*].

As agreed by telephone today, the date for possession will be
[*insert date*], and consequently the date for completion will be
[*insert date*].

A binding contract now exists, but formal documents are being
prepared and they will be forwarded to you for
signing/executing as a deed [*delete as appropriate*] within the
next few days.

Yours faithfully

Copies: Employer
            Quantity surveyor

Letter 103
To consultants, regarding successful tenderer

Dear Sir

Tenders were opened on the [*insert date*] and the successful tenderer was [*insert name*] of [*insert address*].

Work on site is expected to commence on [*insert date*] and you should finalise all your preparations with this date in mind.

I have arranged a meeting, at which the contractor will be present, on the [*insert date*]. Please confirm that you will attend.

Yours faithfully

Letter 104
To unsuccessful tenderers

Dear Sir

I refer to my letter of the [*insert date*] and I confirm that your tender for the above work was not successful.

Tenders received were as follows:

[*List amounts in ascending order. Names of tenderers may also be listed, separately, in alphabetical order unless to do so would make it possible to link tenderers with amounts*].

Yours faithfully

9 Project Planning

Prepare the contract documentation yourself. Do not leave it to the quantity surveyor or to your client's solicitor. Letters of intent can be dangerous, although at times they are inevitable; a valid contract can be concluded unless they are carefully worded. Get expert opinion on the draft letter when you have written it.

Check and make sure that all insurances have been taken out by the appropriate party under the contract. Keep a checklist, particularly for those insurances which are left by the contract to be taken out only if the employer so wishes. Be sure that the contractor has obtained any performance bonds which he is to obtain under the provisions of the contract. It is a sound idea to have a condition precedent written into the contract making it unenforceable unless the bond is in place.

During this stage, all necessary preparations must be made for a start on site and you should take the opportunity to confirm to the contractor any points about the duties of the clerk of works which may otherwise cause trouble later. A number of standard letters are included which deal with some of the common items which should be confirmed before stage K.

Letter 105

To contractor, enclosing the contract documents
Registered Post/Recorded Delivery

Dear Sir

I refer to my letter of the *[insert date]* notifying acceptance of
your tender for the above work. I now have pleasure in
enclosing two copies of the contract documents as follows:

1.   *[Insert name of particular form of building contract
        together with all the official amendment numbers and
        years and any supplements]*.
2.   Priced bills of quantities/specification/Employer's
        Requirements/Contractor's Proposals/Contract Sum
        Analysis *[delete as appropriate]*.
3.   *[Any similar document such as a reduction bill]*.
4.   Drawings numbers *[insert numbers]*.

Please examine the documents carefully, then:

[continued]

Letter 105 continued

---

a. *[If executed as a deed by a corporate body]* Two directors, or one director and the company secretary, must sign the appropriate attestation clause in the printed form of contract. *[If executed as a deed by an individual]* Sign the appropriate attestation clause in the printed form of contract and have the signature witnessed. *[If a deed under seal]* Sign and have witnessed the appropriate attestation clause in the printed form of contract and fix your seal in the place indicated. *[If under hand]* Sign and have witnessed the appropriate attestation clause in the printed form of contract.

b. Initial the printed forms of contract where indicated.

c. Sign and have witnessed the priced bills *[or specification, or Employer's Requirements and Contractor's Proposals and the Contract Sum Analysis]* and each of the drawings as indicated.

Please return all the documents to me and, after completion by the employer, one set will be returned to you.

Yours faithfully

Letter 106
To client, enclosing the contract documents
Registered Post/Recorded Delivery

Dear Sir

I have pleasure in enclosing two copies of the contract documents as follows:

1. *[Insert name of particular form of building contract together with all the official amendment numbers and years and any supplements]*.
2. Priced bills of quantities/specification/Employer's Requirements/Contractor's Proposals/Contract Sum Analysis *[delete as appropriate]*.
3. *[Any similar document such as a reduction bill]*.
4. Drawings numbers *[insert numbers]*.

Please examine the documents carefully, then:

[continued]

Letter 106 continued

a.   [*If executed as a deed by a corporate body*] Two
       directors, or one director and the company secretary
       must sign the appropriate attestation clause in the
       printed form of contract. [*If executed as a deed by an
       individual*] Sign the appropriate attestation clause in the
       printed form of contract and have the signature
       witnessed. [*If a deed under seal*] Sign and have
       witnessed the appropriate attestation clause in the
       printed form of contract and fix your seal in the place
       indicated. [*If under hand*] Sign and have witnessed the
       appropriate attestation clause in the printed form of
       contract.
b.   Initial the printed form of contract where indicated.
c.   Sign and have witnessed the priced bills [*or
       specification, or Employer's Requirements and
       Contractor's Proposals and Contract Sum Analysis*] and
       each of the drawings as indicated.

Please return all the documents to me so that I can date them.

Yours faithfully

Letter 107
To contractor, returning one copy of the contract documents

Dear Sir

I have pleasure in enclosing one copy of the contract documents, duly completed by the employer, for your retention.

Yours faithfully

Letter 108
To client, regarding letter of intent to contractor

Dear Sir

Following your instructions of the [*insert date*] I enclose a draft letter of intent which I propose to send to the successful tenderer.

I should be pleased to have your agreement as soon as possible to avoid delay. If you have any observations, I should be grateful if you would telephone me before [*insert date*].

Yours faithfully

Letter 109
To contractor: letter of intent

Dear Sir

My client [*insert name*], has instructed me to inform you that your tender of the [*insert date*] in the sum of [*insert amount*] for [*insert the nature of the work*] is acceptable and that I intend to prepare the main contract documents for signature subject to my client [*insert the appropriate provisos*].

It is not my client's intention that this letter should be evidence of a binding contract. However, my client is prepared to instruct you to [*insert details of the limited nature of the work required*]. If, for any reason whatsoever, no contract is entered into with you for this work, my client's commitment will be strictly limited to payment for [*insert the limited nature of the work required*].

No other work included in your tender must be carried out without a further written order. No further obligation is placed upon my client and no obligation whatsoever, under any circumstances, is placed upon me.

Yours faithfully

Letter 110a
To contractor regarding insurance
This letter is not suitable for use with MW 80 or GC/Works/1

Dear Sir

I write on behalf of the employer to request you to submit to me insurance policies and premium receipts in accordance with clause 21.1.2 [*substitute '6.2.2' when using IFC 84*] of the contract for inspection by the employer. These documents must be in my hands by no later than [*insert date*].

[*Add, if appropriate:*]

You are further requested to submit to the employer for his approval the name of the insurers with whom you propose to take out insurance under clause 22A [*substitute '6.3A' when using IFC 84 of the contract*]. This information must be in my hands no later than [*insert date*].

[*continued*]

Letter 110a continued

[*Add, if appropriate:*]

Insurance will be required in accordance with clause 21.2.1
[*substitute '6.2.4' when using IFC 84*] and we hereby instruct
you to take out and maintain a joint names policy for the
amount of indemnity specified in the appendix. Before so doing,
please submit to me, for approval by the employer, the name of
the insurers with whom you propose to take out such insurance.

Yours faithfully

Copy: Employer

Letter 110b

To contractor, regarding insurance
This letter is only suitable for use with MW 80

Dear Sir

I write on behalf of the employer to request you to submit to me
insurance policies and premium receipts to show that the
insurances referred to in clauses 6.1 and 6.2 have been taken out
and are in force. These documents, which should include
policies and premium receipts in respect of all sub-contractors,
must be in my hands no later than [*insert date*].

[*Add, if appropriate:*]

You are further requested to submit insurance policies and
premium receipts to show that the insurances referred to in
clause 6.3A have been taken out and are in force. Note that
such insurances must be taken out in the joint names of the
employer and yourself and must be for the full reinstatement
value plus [*insert percentage*] as stated in clause 6.3A to cover
professional fees. These documents must be in my hands no
later than [*insert date*].

Yours faithfully

Copy: Employer

Letter 110c
To contractor, regarding insurance
This letter is only suitable for use with GC/Works/1

Dear Sir

I write on behalf of the employer to request you to submit to me

[*Add either:*]

copies of insurances in respect of employer's liability, loss or damage to the works and things for which you are responsible under the terms of the contract and insurance against personal injury to any persons and loss or damage to property arising from or in connection with the works, all in accordance with clauses 8(1), 8(2) and 8(3) of the contract.

[*Or:*]

copies of insurance in respect of employer's liability and insurances in accordance with the summary of essential insurance requirements attached to the abstract of particulars, all as clauses 8(1)(a) and 8(3) of the contract.

Yours faithfully

Letter 111a
To client, regarding insurance
This letter is not suitable for use with MW 80 or GC/Works/1

Dear Sir

I enclose a letter which I sent to the contractor regarding insurances. The contents are self-explanatory. When the contractor submits the requested information, you should pass it immediately to your insurance broker for his comments. If you will ask your broker to send a copy of his comments to me, I will pass them to the contractor.

[*Add, if appropriate:*]

The contract requires you to take out all risks insurance cover in the joint names of the contractor and yourself under clause 22B/22C [*delete as appropriate and substitute '6.3B' or '6.3C' when using IFC 84*] for the full reinstatement value of the works plus [*insert percentage*] as stated in the appendix to cover professional fees [*add, if appropriate*] together with joint names insurance against specified perils for existing structures and contents. In certain circumstances, it may be possible to extend your existing insurance cover. I enclose the relevant extracts from the contract and you should speak to your own insurance broker without delay so that cover is effective from [*insert date*]. Please let me know when you have arranged cover so that I can notify the contractor.

Yours faithfully

Letter 111b
To client, regarding insurance
This letter is only suitable for use with MW 80

Dear Sir

I enclose a letter which I have sent to the contractor regarding insurances. The contents are self-explanatory. When the contractor submits the requested information, you should pass it immediately to your own insurance broker for his comments. If you will ask your broker to send a copy of his comments to me, I will pass them to the contractor.

[*Add, if appropriate:*]

The contract requires you to take out insurance cover in the joint names of the contractor and yourself under clause 6.3B against loss or damage to the existing structures and contents, and to the works. In certain circumstances, it may be possible to extend your existing insurance cover. I enclose the relevant extracts from the contract and you should speak to your broker without delay so that cover is effective from [*insert date*]. Please let me know when you have arranged cover so that I can notify the contractor.

Yours faithfully

Letter 111c

To client, regarding insurance
This letter is only suitable for use with GC/Works/1

Dear Sir

I enclose a letter which I have sent to the contractor regarding insurances. The contents are self-explanatory. When the contractor submits the requested information, you should pass it to your own insurance broker for his comments. If you will ask your broker to write directly to me, I will pass the comments to the contractor.

Yours faithfully

Letter 112

To contractor, regarding insurance policies
This letter is not suitable for use with MW 80 or GC/Works/1

Dear Sir

I return herewith the insurance policies numbers [*insert numbers*] and premium receipts numbers [*insert numbers*] in respect of clause 21.1.2 [*substitute '6.2.2' when using IFC 84*] of the contract. The employer has completed his inspection [*add, if appropriate:*] and he has the following comments to make: [*insert the comments received from the employer's brokers*].

[*Add, if appropriate:*]

Your proposal to take out insurance with [*insert name of proposed insurers*] in accordance with the requirements of clause 22A [*substitute '6.3A' when using IFC 84*] is approved by the employer. Note that such insurances must be taken out in the joint names of the employer and yourself and must be for the full reinstatement value plus [*insert percentage*] as stated in the appendix to cover professional fees. The policy or policies and receipts for premiums paid must be deposited with the employer no later than [*insert date*].

[*continued*]

Letter 112 continued

[*Add, if appropriate*]

Your proposal to take out insurance with [*insert name of proposed insurers*] in accordance with the requirements of clause 21.2.1 [*substitute '6.2.4' when using IFC 84*] is approved by the employer. Please proceed to take out insurance in the joint names of the employer and yourself for the amount of indemnity specified in the appendix. The policy or policies and receipts for premiums paid must be deposited with the employer no later than [*insert date*].

Yours faithfully

Letter 113

To contractor, regarding liquidated damages insurance
This letter is not suitable for use with MW 80 or GC/Works/1

Dear Sir

[*Either:*]

Although it is stated in the appendix that clause 22D [*substitute
'6.3D' when using IFC 84*] insurance may be required, I confirm
that no such insurance is required.

[*Or:*]

I should be pleased if you would obtain a quotation for
insurance to which clause 22D [*substitute '6.3D' when using IFC
84*] refers for the time period stated in the appendix. The
insurance must be on an agreed value basis. Please let me know
without delay if you reasonably require any further information
to obtain such quotation.

Yours faithfully

Letter 114

To contractor, after receiving liquidated damages insurance quotation
This letter is not suitable for use with MW 80 or GC/Works/1

Dear Sir

Thank you for forwarding the quotation you have received in connection with the insurance to which clause 22D [*substitute '6.3D' when using IFC 84*] refers.

[*Then, either:*]

I have received instructions from the employer that he does not wish you to accept the quotation in this instance.

[*Or:*]

I have received instructions from the employer that he wishes you to accept the quotation and I should be pleased if you would forthwith take out and maintain the relevant policy and send it to me for deposit with the employer together with the premium receipt therefor and any relevant endorsement or endorsements thereof and the premium receipts therefor.

Yours faithfully

Letter 115
To contractor, regarding performance bond

Dear Sir

Page [*insert number*] item [*insert item reference*] of the
contract bills [*or specification*] requires you to provide a
performance bond in the sum of [*insert amount*].

Please arrange the bond immediately and, on completion, let me
have the original document, not a copy, which will be lodged
with the employer until after practical
completion/completion/completion of making good defects
[*delete as appropriate*] of the works.

Yours faithfully

Letter 116
To client, at the beginning of the building contract

Dear Sir

I am taking the opportunity to write to you before the contractor takes possession of the site and commences work. There are a number of points worth emphasising, because they have an important effect on the proper and efficient progress of the work and they concern you as employer under the contract:

1.	Until the contract is executed, I am required to act solely as your agent within the limits laid down by the terms of my appointment. Thereafter, although I continue to act for you as before, I owe you the additional duty to administer the contract fairly between the parties. This means that I must make any decisions under the contract strictly in accordance with the terms of the contract.

2.	The contract obliges me to issue all certificates at the appropriate time and to use my professional judgment in so doing. An important type of certificate I have to issue is the financial certificate which stipulates the amount of money due to the contractor. These certificates are issued at [*insert frequency*] intervals during the period that work is in progress and

[*continued*]

Letter 116 continued

occasionally thereafter. You have a maximum of
[*insert number*] days from the date of each certificate to
get your payment to the contractor. The importance of
paying the contractor the full amount indicated on the
certificate within the period allowed cannot be stressed
too much. Failure to honour certificates within the time
limit allows the contractor to commence the procedure
for determining his employment. The result of this
would be disastrous to the contract in terms of both time
and money.

3.   If the contractor communicates with you by letter,
telephone or personal visit, please refer him to me and
let me know immediately. It is not advisable for you to
answer any of his queries or make decisions regarding
the contract without consulting me. It could be costly.
If there are any matters requiring your decision, I will
refer them to you as they arise, with my observations.

4.   If you wish to visit the site from time to time, to see the
work in progress, please let me know so that I can make
myself available to accompany you on each occasion to
take care of any points which may arise. I will, of
course, keep you informed on a regular basis regarding
the progress of the work and the financial situation.

Yours faithfully

Letter 117
To clerk of works, on appointment

Dear Sir

My client, [*insert name*], has confirmed your appointment as clerk of works for the above contract. I should be pleased if you would call at this office on [*insert date*] at [*insert time*] to be briefed on the project and to collect your copies of drawings, bills of quantities [*or specification*], weekly report forms and daily diary.

It is anticipated that the contractor will take possession of the site on the [*insert date*]. You are expected to be present on site [*insert periods during which the clerk of works is expected to be present*]. According to the contractor's programme, all site accommodation will be completed by day [*insert day number*] and I should be glad if you would check that it is in accordance with the contract.

Your duties will be as described in the contract clause 12 [*substitute '3.10' when using IFC 84, '4' when using GC/Works/1 or 'specification' as appropriate*] a copy of which is enclosed for your reference. In particular, I wish to draw your attention to the following:

[*continued*]

Letter 117 continued

1.   You will be expected to inspect all workmanship and materials to ensure conformity with the contract requirements. Any defects must be drawn to the attention of the person-in-charge [*substitute 'agent' when using GC/Works/1*], to whom you should address all comments. If any defects are left unremedied for twenty-four hours or if they are of a major or fundamental nature, you must inform me immediately by telephone. Do not issue any written directions to the contractor.

2.   Although it is common practice for clerks of works to mark defective work on site, the contract gives you no such power. You must not in any way deface materials on site whether or not they are incorporated into the structure.

3.   It is not my policy to issue lists of defects to the contractor before practical completion [*substitute 'completion' when using GC/Works/1*]. Commonly called 'snagging lists', they may be misinterpreted and give rise to disputes. They should be compiled by the person-in-charge [*substitute 'agent' when using GC/Works/1*]. Please confine your remarks to the contractor to oral comments.

4.   The architect is the only person empowered to issue instructions to the contractor.

5.   You are not empowered to vary work or materials or design. Refer all queries to me.

[*continued*]

Letter 117 continued

---

6.   Complete the weekly report sheets, paying especial
      attention to [*insert as required*] and send them to me
      each Monday.
7.   Complete the diary as fully as possible.
8.   Remember that your weekly report sheets and diary
      may be called in evidence in the case of a dispute. Bear
      this in mind when making entries.
9.   Remember that, although I may call upon you to carry
      out various tasks in relation to the contract, your
      primary duty is to the employer as inspector on the
      works. You have no duty to the contractor under the
      provisions of the contract, but you have a duty under the
      general law not to make careless statements.

I hope you achieve the kind of relationship with the contractor
on which successful completion of the contract depends so much.
Do not hesitate to contact me if you are in doubt about
anything.

Yours faithfully

Letter 118
To contractor, noting the authority of the clerk of works

Dear Sir

A clerk of works has been appointed for the above contract. His name is [*insert name*] and he is experienced in work of this type. I hope that you will build up a successful relationship over the coming months.

The clerk of works will be on site during the whole/part of the week only [*delete as appropriate*]. His duties are as laid down in the contract clause 12 [*substitute '3.10' when using IFC 84, '4' when using GC/Works/1 or 'specification' as appropriate*]. I hope it will be helpful if I emphasise that he is acting as an inspector of materials and workmanship; he is not empowered to issue instructions. Although I expect that he will be ready to give his opinion, if requested, on any points which may arise during construction, the responsibility for carrying out the works in accordance with the contract remains yours. Please note especially that the clerk of works is in no way a substitute for your own supervisory staff. The clerk of works owes his duty to the employer although he is under my direction.

[*continued*]

Letter 118 continued

I have informed him that he must not make any marks on the
works to indicate defective materials, because I know this can be
a source of annoyance. No snagging lists will be issued. This
should remove any misunderstandings regarding the extent of
defective work. If the clerk of works notices any workmanship
or materials not in accordance with the contract, he will point it
out on site, note it in his diary and report it to me. I trust that it
will be unnecessary for me to issue specific instructions regarding
such matters. The failure of the clerk of works to notice
defective work does not, of course, affect your own obligations
under the contract.

If you are in any doubt regarding the contents of this letter,
please do not hesitate to write or telephone me for clarification.

Yours faithfully

Copy: Clerk of works

Letter 119
To contractor, regarding extension of authority of the clerk of works

Dear Sir

I should be pleased if you would note that the clerk of works is my authorised representative for the purposes of clause [*insert clause number*] of the contract and for that purpose alone.

[*Set out a brief description of the authority of the clerk of works under the clause*]

This extension of the authority of the clerk of works will apply until further notice, but note that his other duties remain unaffected.

Yours faithfully

Copies: Clerk of works
Quantity surveyor

Letter 120
To contractor, naming authorised representatives

Dear Sir

This is to formally let you know that the architect's authorised representatives for all the purposes of the contract are:

[*List representatives, giving names and positions in the firm*]

This arrangement will apply until further notice.

Yours faithfully

for and on behalf of
[*insert name in the contract which should be the firm name*]

Copies: Employer
Consultants
Clerk of works

Letter 121
To contractor, regarding the issue of instructions

Dear Sir

It seems timely to draw your attention to the fact that the architect is the only person authorised to issue instructions under this contract.

All other instructions, from whatsoever source, are of no effect unless confirmed by the architect in writing.

The restriction applies to all consultants engaged by the employer on this project. If, despite this letter, you receive an instruction from some person other than the architect, it should be referred to me immediately and you should neither act nor forebear from acting on account of the instruction.

Yours faithfully

Copies: Employer
Quantity surveyor
Consultants
Clerk of works

Letter 122a
To contractor, regarding sub-letting
This letter is not suitable for use with CD 81

Dear Sir

I am writing to draw your attention to clause 19.2.2 [*substitute '3.2' when using IFC 84 or MW 80, or '62(1)' when using GC/Works/1*] of the contract which prohibits sub-letting any part of the works without my consent [*add, if using GC/Works/1:*] unless the employer accepted a sub-letting proposal prior to the award of the contract.

Will you please note that, before giving my consent, I will require you to inform me of the names of the proposed sub-contractors and the parts of the works you wish to sub-let.

Yours faithfully

Letter 122b

To contractor, regarding sub-letting
This letter is only suitable for use with CD 81

Dear Sir

I am writing to draw your attention to clauses 18.2.1 and 18.2.3 of the contract which prohibit sub-letting of any part of the works or the design of any part of the works respectively without my consent.

Will you please note that, before giving my consent, I will require you to inform me of the names of the proposed sub-contractors and the parts of the works you wish to sub-let or of which you wish to sub-let the design. If I give my consent for the sub-letting of design under clause 18.2.3, such consent will not affect in any way your obligation under clause 2.5.

Yours faithfully

Letter 123
To contractor, if architect is employee of the employer

Dear Sir

I am taking this opportunity of writing to you before work begins on site in order to make my position clear as employee of the employer named in the contract and also as the architect named in the same contract.

The extent of my authority is laid down in the contract and I have no general power of agency to bind the employer outside its express terms. If I have to make decisions under the contract terms, I will decide all such matters impartially between the parties. If I have cause to write to you on behalf of the employer, I will clearly so state.

Yours faithfully

10 Operations on Site

This stage involves a considerable amount of letter writing if the project is other than very minor. A number of matters can be dealt with by standard letters. The major items are procedures if the contractor fails to take out insurance or fails to comply with instructions, performance specified work, extensions of time, liquidated damages, loss and/or expense, determination and arbitration, but there are many other items throughout the construction phase when standard letters are useful.

An attempt has been made to arrange the letters in some kind of reasonable order while acknowledging that many of them could be sent at any time. Thus, after letters about failure to insure, come possession of the site, then numerous letters about compliance with instructions, extensions, etc.

It is anticipated that you are quite capable of choosing the correct letter for a given situation and, indeed, amending it to suit your own particular requirements.

Letter 124a

To contractor, if he fails to maintain insurance cover
This letter is only suitable for use with JCT 80 and CD 81

Dear Sir

I refer to my telephone conversation with your [*insert name*]
this morning and confirm that you are unable to produce the
insurance policy, premium receipts or other documentary
evidence that the insurance required by clause
21.1.1.1/22A.1/21.2.1/22D.1 [*delete as appropriate*] is being
maintained.

In view of the importance of the insurance and without prejudice
to your liabilities [*if a clause 21.1.1.1 failure, insert: 'under
clause 20 of the conditions of contract'*], the employer is
arranging to exercise his rights under clause 21.1.3/22A.2/21.2.4
['*21.2.3' when using CD 81*]/22D.4 [*delete as appropriate*]
immediately. [*In respect of clauses 21.1.1.1 and 22A.1 add:*]
Any sum or sums payable by him in respect of premiums will be
deducted from any monies due or to become due to you or will
be recovered from you as a debt. [*In respect of clauses 21.2.1
and 22D.1 add:*] Any sum or sums payable by him in respect of
premiums will not be included in the adjustment of the contract
sum.

Yours faithfully

Letter 124b
To contractor, if he fails to maintain insurance cover
This letter is only suitable for use with IFC 84

Dear Sir

I refer to my telephone conversation with your [*insert name*] this morning and confirm that you are unable to produce the insurance policy, premium receipts or other documentary evidence that the insurance required by clause 6.2.1/6.3A.1/6.2.4/6.3D.1 [*delete as appropriate*] is being maintained.

In view of the importance of the insurance and without prejudice to your liabilities [*if a clause 6.2.1 failure, insert 'under clause 6.1 of the conditions of contract'*], the employer is arranging to exercise his rights under clause 6.2.3/6.3A.2/6.2.4/6.3D.4 [*delete as appropriate*] immediately. [*In respect of clauses 6.2.1 and 6.3A.1 add:*] Any sum or sums payable by him in respect of premiums will be deducted from any monies due or to become due to you or will be recovered from you as a debt. [*In respect of clauses 6.2.4 and 6.3D.1 add:*] Any sum or sums payable by him in respect of premiums will not be included in the adjustment of the contract sum.

Yours faithfully

Copies: Employer
Quantity Surveyor

Letter 124c

To contractor, if he fails to maintain insurance cover
This letter is only suitable for use with MW 80

Dear Sir

I refer to my telephone conversation with your *[insert name]* this morning and confirm that you are unable to produce such evidence as the employer may reasonably require in accordance with clause 6.4 of the conditions of contract that the insurances referred to in clause 6.1/6.2/6.3A *[delete as appropriate]* have been taken out and are in force.

This is a clear breach of contract on your part and, in view of the importance of the insurance and without prejudice to your liabilities under clause 6.1/6.2/6.3A *[delete as appropriate]*, the employer is arranging to take out the appropriate insurances on your behalf. Any sum or sums payable by him in respect of premiums will be deducted from any monies due or to become due to you or will be recovered from you as a debt.

Yours faithfully

Copies: Employer
Quantity surveyor (if appointed)

Letter 124d

To contractor, if he fails to maintain insurance cover
This letter is only suitable for use with GC/Works/1

Dear Sir

I refer to my telephone conversation with your [*insert name*] this morning and confirm that you are unable to produce the insurance policy, premium receipts or other documentary evidence that the insurance required by clause 8 is being maintained.

In view of the importance of the insurance and without prejudice to your liabilities under clause 8 of the conditions of contract, the employer is arranging to exercise his rights under clause 8(4). The cost of effecting the appropriate insurance cover will be deducted from any advance payment due to you under the contract.

Yours faithfully

Copies: Employer
         Quantity Surveyor (if appointed)

Letter 125a
To client, if contractor fails to maintain insurance cover
This letter is only suitable for use with JCT 80 or CD 81

Dear Sir

The contractor is unable to provide evidence that he is maintaining the insurance cover required by clause 21.1.1.1/22A.1/21.2.1/22D.1 [*delete as appropriate*] of the conditions of contract.

In view of the importance of the insurance, I have taken action on your behalf, under clause 21.1.3/22A.2/21.2.4 ['*21.2.3*' *when using CD 81*] /22D.4 [*delete as appropriate*] and instructed your broker to provide the necessary cover effective from today. [*In respect of clauses 21.1.1.1 and 22A.1 add:*] You are entitled to deduct the amount of the premium from your next payment to the contractor or, alternatively, you may wish to recover it as a debt. [*In respect of clauses 21.2.1 and 22D.1 add:*] Naturally, the amount of your premium will not be included in the adjustment of the contract sum.

Yours faithfully

Letter 125b

To client, if contractor fails to maintain insurance cover
This letter is only suitable for use with IFC 84

Dear Sir

The contractor is unable to provide evidence that he is maintaining the insurance cover required by clause 6.2.1/6.3A.1/6.2.4/6.3D.1 [*delete as appropriate*] of the conditions of contract.

In view of the importance of the insurance, I have taken action on your behalf, under clause 6.2.3/6.3A.2/6.2.4/6.3D.4 [*delete as appropriate*], and instructed your broker to provide the necessary cover effective from today. [*In respect of clauses 6.2.1 and 6.3A.1 add:*] You are entitled to deduct the amount of the premium from your next payment to the contractor or, alternatively, you may wish to recover it as a debt. [*In respect of clauses 6.2.4 and 6.3D.1 add:*] Naturally, the amount of your premium will not be included in the adjustment of the contract sum.

Yours faithfully

Letter 125c
To client, if contractor fails to maintain insurance cover
This letter is only suitable for use with MW 80

Dear Sir

The contractor is unable to provide evidence in accordance with clause 6.4 of the conditions of contract that he is maintaining the insurance cover required by clause 6.1/6.2/6.3A [*delete as appropriate*] of the conditions of contract.

In view of the importance of the insurance, I have taken action on your behalf and instructed your broker to provide the necessary cover effective from today. Although the terms of the contract make no express provision for you to act on the contractor's default, it is my opinion that, in this instance, you are entitled to deduct the cost of the premium from your next payment to the contractor.

A copy of my letter to the contractor, dated [*insert date*], is enclosed for your information.

Yours faithfully

Letter 125d

To client, if contractor fails to maintain insurance cover
This letter is only suitable for use with GC/Works/1

Dear Sir

The contractor is unable to provide evidence that he is maintaining the insurance cover required by clause 8 of the conditions of contract.

In view of the importance of the insurance, I have taken action on your behalf, under clause 8(4), and instructed your broker to provide the necessary cover effective from today. You are entitled to deduct the cost of so insuring from any advance payment due to the contractor under the contract.

Yours faithfully

Letter 126

To client's insurance broker, if contractor fails to maintain insurance cover

Dear Sir

I am writing to you in connection with the above project about which my client [*insert name*] has already consulted you. I am writing separately to my client and sending him a copy of this letter.

The contractor has failed to maintain/take out [*delete as appropriate*] insurance cover as required by clause [*insert one of 21.1.1.1/22A.1/21.2.1/22D.1 when using JCT 80, insert one of 6.2.1/6.3A.1/6.2.4/6.3D.1 when using IFC 84, insert 6.1/6.2/6.3A when using MW 80 or insert 8 when using GC/Works/1*] of the conditions of contract and it is, therefore, necessary that my client takes out such insurance himself. The relevant extract from the contract is enclosed. Please arrange insurance cover immediately. The premium will be paid by my client, but you should let me know the amount so that it can be recovered from the contractor.

Yours faithfully

Copies: Employer
        Quantity Surveyor

Letter 127
To contractor, confirming possession of the site

Dear Sir

I confirm that the above site was available for you to take possession on the *[insert date]*, which is the date stated in the contract.

Yours faithfully

Copy: Employer

Letter 128

Draft letter from employer to contractor, deferring possession of the site

This letter is not suitable for use with MW 80 or GC/Works/1

Dear Sir

[*If length of deferment is known*]

I hereby give you notice in accordance with clause 23.1.2 [*substitute '2.2' when using IFC 84*] of the conditions of contract that I defer giving possession of the site for [*insert period which should not exceed six weeks*]. You may take possession of the site on [*insert date*].

[*If length of deferment is not known*]

I hereby give you notice in accordance with clause 23.1.2 [*substitute '2.2' when using IFC 84*] of the conditions of contract that I defer giving possession of the site for a period which will not exceed [*insert period named in the appendix*]. I will write to you again when I have a definite date for possession.

Yours faithfully

Copies: Architect
        Quantity Surveyor
        Consultants
        Clerk of works

Letter 129
To contractor, if Contractor's Statement is deficient
This letter is only suitable for use with JCT 80

Dear Sir

Thank you for your letter of the [*insert date*] with which you enclosed a copy of your Contractor's Statement in respect of the performance specified work identified in the appendix as [*insert brief description of the work as noted in the appendix*].

It is my opinion that such Statement is deficient adequately to explain your proposals, because [*insert reason why it is deficient*].

Take this letter as written notice under clause 42.5 of the conditions of contract requiring you to amend such Statement so that it will no longer be deficient as noted above.

[*Add, if appropriate:*]

This letter also serves as written notice under clause 42.6.

Yours faithfully

Letter 130

To contractor, requiring the Analysis
This letter is only suitable for use with JCT 80

Dear Sir

No analysis of the portion of the contract sum which relates to performance specified work is provided in the contract bills. Therefore, in accordance with clause 42.13 of the conditions of contract, I require you to provide such an analysis (the 'Analysis') within 14 days of the date of this letter.

Yours faithfully

Letter 131

To contractor, if architect finds discrepancy in Contractor's Statement
This letter is only suitable for use with JCT 80

Dear Sir

In accordance with clause 2.4.2 of the conditions of contract, I bring to your attention the following discrepancies which I have discovered:

[*List, giving precise details*]

Please correct the Statement to remove the discrepancy and inform me in writing of the correction you have made. Note that such correction must be at no cost to the employer.

Yours faithfully

Letter 132

To contractor, if the architect finds a divergence between the
Contractor's Statement and statutory requirements
This letter is only suitable for use with JCT 80

Dear Sir

I have found what appears to be a divergence between your
Contractor's Statement and statutory requirements and, in
accordance with clause 6.1.6 of the conditions of contract, I
hereby give you written notice as follows:

[*Insert details of the divergence*]

Please inform me in writing of your proposed amendment to
remove the divergence so that I can issue instructions without
delay. [*If clauses 6.1.7 or 42.15 are not applicable, add:*] Your
compliance with such instructions will be without cost to the
employer.

Yours faithfully

Letter 133
To contractor, if architect finds discrepancy within the Employer's Requirements
This letter is only suitable for use with CD 81

Dear Sir

I note the following discrepancy within the Employer's Requirements [*insert details*].

[*Then either:*]

Your Contractor's Proposals [*insert reference to item*] deal with the matter and, therefore, they prevail in accordance with clause 2.4.1 of the conditions of contract. There will be no adjustment to the contract sum.

[*Or:*]

Your Contractor's Proposals do not deal with the matter and, therefore, I should be pleased if you would comply with clause 2.4.1 of the conditions of contract and inform me in writing of your proposed amendment to deal with the discrepancy so that the employer may either agree or decide how to deal with the discrepancy.

Yours faithfully

Letter 134

To contractor, if architect finds a discrepancy within the Contractor's
Proposals
This letter is only suitable for use with CD 81

Dear Sir

I note the following discrepancy within the Contractor's
Proposals [*insert details*].

In accordance with clause 2.4.2 of the conditions of contract I
should be pleased to receive your proposed amendment to
remove the discrepancy so that the employer may either decide
between the discrepant items or may accept your proposed
amendment. Your compliance with such decision or acceptance
will be without cost to the employer.

Yours faithfully

Letter 135

To contractor, requesting consent to the addition of persons to the list under clause 19.3
This letter is only suitable for use with JCT 80

Dear Sir

On behalf of the employer, [*insert name*], I hereby formally request your consent, as required under clause 19.3.2.1 of the conditions of contract, to the addition of [*insert name*] of [*insert address*] to the list of persons named in the contract bills reference [*insert reference*] to carry out [*insert description of the work as given in the contract bills*].

Yours faithfully

Letter 136
To contractor, if he sub-lets without architect's consent

Dear Sir

I am informed that you have sub-let [*insert part of the works sub-let*] to [*insert name of sub-contractor*].

Because, I have not given my consent, your action is a breach of contract and it must cease forthwith. Please confirm, by return, that you will comply with this letter. [*add, except when using MW 80:*] I have no wish to advise the employer to use his powers under clause 27.2.1.4 [*substitute '7.1(d)' when using IFC 84 or '56(1)' when using GC/Works/1*].

Yours faithfully

Letter 137a
To contractor, regarding employer's licensees
This letter is not suitable for use with MW 80 or GC/Works/1

Dear Sir

The employer is anxious to arrange [*insert the nature of the work*] commencing on [*insert date*]. Because this work does not form part of the contract and the contract documents do not provide for the employer to carry out the work himself, he has instructed me to request your consent to the carrying out of such work by persons employed directly by the employer.

This request is made in accordance with the provisions of clause 29.2 [*substitute '3.11' when using IFC 84*].

Yours faithfully

Letter 137b
To contractor, regarding employer's licensees
This letter is only suitable for use with GC/Works/1

Dear Sir

The employer instructs me to inform you that, in accordance with clause 65(1) of the conditions of contract, he intends to carry out [*insert the nature of the work*] using his own directly employed contractors. Work will commence on [*insert date*].

Please inform me immediately if you consider that the work should not proceed as indicated.

Yours faithfully

Letter 138
To client, enclosing report on progress

Dear Sir

I have pleasure in enclosing my report number [*insert number*] giving details of the progress of this project. If you wish me to enlarge upon any part of the report, I shall be happy to do so.

[*If this is the first time a progress report is being sent, add:*]

You will receive further progress reports in this form at [*insert period*] intervals. If there is any aspect of the report on which you wish me to elaborate in the future, please let me know.

Yours faithfully

Letter 139
To persons affected, enclosing extract of minutes

Dear Sir

At a meeting held on the *[insert date]* between *[insert names of principal participants]*, it was resolved:

[Insert minute, including reference number, then either]

I should be pleased if you would take the appropriate action.

[Or:]

I should be pleased to receive your comments.

[Or:]

Please note the minute in your records.

Yours faithfully

Letter 140

To originator of minutes, if architect disagrees with contents

Dear Sir

I have considered the minutes of the meeting held on the [*insert date*] which I received today and I have the following comments:

[*Insert list of comments*]

Please arrange to have these comments published at the next meeting and inserted in the appropriate place in the minutes.

Yours faithfully

*Copies: All present at the meeting and all included in the
          circulation list*

Letter 141a
To client, if disagreeing with former architect's decisions
This letter is not suitable for use with CD 81

Dear Sir

I have examined all the drawings and documents handed to me
on appointment and I have visited site and spoken to the
contractor and the clerk of works.

I find myself unable to agree with the following decisions of the
former architect:

[*List all matters with which you disagree*]

When you have had time to study these matters, I suggest we
should meet to discuss ways of dealing with them. [*Add, if using
JCT 80, IFC 84 or MW 80:*] Article 3 of the contract prevents
me from disregarding or overruling any certificate or instruction
given by the architect previously engaged to administer this
contract.

Yours faithfully

Letter 141b

To contractor client, if disagreeing with former architect's decisions
This letter is only suitable for use with CD 81

Dear Sir

I have examined all the drawings and documents handed to me on appointment and I have visited site. I note that the Employer's Requirements contain a substantial number of relatively detailed drawings produced by the employer's consultant. There are a number of matters which give me cause for concern, but presumably there is little which can be done about it at this stage:

[*List all matters with which you disagree*]

When you have had time to study these matters, I suggest we should meet to discuss ways of dealing with them.

Yours faithfully

Letter 142
To contractor, on receipt of master programme

Dear Sir

Thank you for your letter of the [*insert date*] with which you enclosed two copies of your master programme. My comments are as follows:

[*List comments as questions, not as instructions to change particular parts of the programme*]

I should be pleased if you would reconsider your programme in the light of my comments, but you must not take such comments or lack of comment to indicate approval to the programme in part or in whole. The organisation and method of working and the times allocated to particular activities are your responsibility to carry out within the constraints laid down by the drawings and bills of quantities [*or specification*].

Your master programme is only received as an indication of your intentions. The use of the programme as evidence in any future claim for extension of time <u>or loss and/or expense</u>[1] is subject to my discretion.

Yours faithfully

[1 *Omit when using MW 80*]

Letter 143
To contractor, if architect asked to check setting out

Dear Sir

Thank you for your letter of the [*insert date*].

The setting out is your responsibility <u>under the contract</u>[1]. In my opinion, you have been provided with all necessary dimensions and information to enable you to discharge that responsibility. Any inspection I may decide to carry out will not remove any of your obligations.

Yours faithfully

[1 *Omit this phrase when using MW 80*]

Letter 144

To contractor, requiring reasonable proof that the nominated sub-contractors have been paid
This letter is only suitable for use with JCT 80

Dear Sir

I enclose my interim certificate number [*insert number*] dated [*insert date*] together with direction number [*insert number*] in respect of the amounts included for each nominated sub-contractor.

Please note that, in accordance with clause 35.13.3 you must provide reasonable proof, before the issue of the next interim certificate, that such sub-contract amounts have been duly discharged in accordance with sub-contract NSC/C.

Yours faithfully

Letter 145

To client, if contractor fails to provide reasonable proof of payment to sub-contractors
This letter is only suitable for use with JCT 80

Dear Sir

In accordance with clause 35.13.5.2 of the conditions of contract, I hereby certify that the contractor has failed to provide me with reasonable proof that he has discharged the amount of [*insert amount*] included in my certificate number [*insert number*] dated [*insert date*] in respect of [*insert the name or names of the nominated sub-contractors concerned*].

Yours faithfully

Copies: Nominated sub-contractor
Quantity surveyor
Contractor

Letter 146

To client, if clause 35.13.5.1 certificate issued
This letter is only suitable for use with JCT 80

Dear Sir

I enclose my certificate dated [*insert date*] issued in accordance with clause 35.13.5.1.

In accordance with clause 35.13.5.2 you should pay the sum of [*insert amount*] directly to [*insert name of nominated sub-contractor*] no later than fourteen days from the date of my next interim certificate. You are entitled to reduce the amount payable to the contractor accordingly.

Yours faithfully

Letter 147
To contractor, confirmed acceptance under clause 13A
This letter is only suitable for use with JCT 80

Dear Sir

We refer to your quotation, pursuant to clause 13A of the conditions of contract, dated [*insert date*]. I write in accordance with clause 13A.3.2 of the contract and confirm the following:

1.   The employer has accepted your quotation.
2.   You are to carry out the variation to which the quotation relates.
3.   The contract sum is to be adjusted by the addition/omission [*delete as appropriate*] of [*insert amount*] which takes account of amounts to which clauses 13A.2.3 and 13A.2.4 refer.
4.   The revised date for completion is [*insert date*]. [*Add, if relevant:*] The revised period for completion of [*insert name of nominated sub-contract*] is [*insert period*].
5.   You must accept any clause 3.3A of NSC/C quotation which is included in the quotation for which this letter has been issued.

Yours faithfully

Letter 148
To contractor, if he submits drawings
This letter is not suitable for use with CD 81

Dear Sir

Thank you for your letter dated [*insert date*] with which you enclosed two copies of each of drawings numbers [*insert numbers*].

[*Either:*]

I return one copy of each drawing herewith without comment.

[*Or:*]

My comments are as follows: [*list comments*]

[*Then:*]

It is your responsibility under the contract to supply these drawings and to co-ordinate them and all other documents required to execute the works. This letter must not be construed so as to relieve you of that responsibility. [*insert, if appropriate: 'and my comments are so restricted'*]. I have retained one copy of the drawings for my records.

Yours faithfully

Letter 149
To contractor, if he submits drawings under supplementary provision S2
This letter is only suitable for use with CD 81

Dear Sir

Thank you for your letter dated [*insert date*] with which you enclosed two copies of each of drawings numbers [*insert numbers*].

[*Either:*]

I return one copy of each drawing herewith without comment.

[*Or:*]

My comments are as follows: [*list comments*]

[*Then:*]

It is your responsibility to design the works. That responsibility includes the checking and co-ordination of all drawings required to execute the works. This letter must not be construed so as to relieve you of that responsibility. Neither is it to be construed as an instruction of any kind. My comments are so restricted and your attention is drawn to the provisions of supplementary provision S2.2 in that regard. I have retained one copy of the drawings for my records.

Yours faithfully

Letter 150
To contractor, if letter not understood

Dear Sir

Thank you for your letter of the [*insert date*].

After reading the contents several times, I am afraid that I find the meaning obscure. If I attempted to answer the letter as it stands, I should be merely guessing what you required of me. Rather than waste time on a fruitless exercise, I should be glad if you would rephrase the letter so that I can give it proper consideration.

Yours faithfully

Letter 151
To contractor, pending detailed reply

Dear Sir

Thank you for your letter of the [*insert date*].

In view of the complex nature of the contents, I am unable to reply in detail immediately. I will give careful consideration to the points you make and write to you again in due course. This letter is not to be taken as agreement, express or implied, to the whole or any part of your letter.

Yours faithfully

Letter 152

To contractor, requesting samples
This letter is only suitable for use with CD 81

Dear Sir

I note that you are about to commence work on [*describe the portion of work in question*] and I draw your attention to the fact that you have not yet complied with paragraph [*insert reference*] of the Employer's Requirements/Contractor's Proposals [*delete as appropriate*] which requires you to provide samples of [*insert material*].

I should be pleased to have these samples forthwith. If you proceed with the work before providing such samples, you will be in breach of clause 8.6 on the conditions of contract.

Yours faithfully

Letter 153
To contractor, regarding samples

Dear Sir

I have examined/had tests carried out on [*delete as appropriate*]
the samples of [*insert material*] which you delivered to this
office on the [*insert date*] and which were marked [*insert
reference number*] for identification purposes.

I have no comment to make on the standard of
workmanship/quality of materials [*delete as appropriate*] as
demonstrated by the samples in accordance with bills of
quantities [*or specification, or Employer's Requirements or
Contractor's Proposals when using CD 81*] reference [*insert
reference*]. One sample is being retained in this office and the
remaining samples are being sent to site in the care of the clerk
of works.

Yours faithfully

Copy: Clerk of works

Letter 154
To contractor, regarding failure of samples

Dear Sir

I have examined/had tests carried out on [*delete as appropriate*] the samples of [*insert material*] which you delivered to this office on the [*insert date*] and which were marked [*insert reference*] for identification purposes.

The samples are not satisfactory, because they are not in accordance with the contract. I refer you to [*insert appropriate reference in drawings, bills of quantities or specification, or Employer's Requirements or Contractor's Proposals when using CD 81*]. Further samples of the proper quality must be submitted forthwith.

Yours faithfully

Copy: Clerk of works

Letter 155
To manufacturer, if problems with product on site

Dear Sir

I specified your [*insert name of product*] on the above project. Work has reached [*insert stage*] and I am concerned to note that [*insert nature of problem*].

[*Add one of the following:*]

A site meeting is being held at [*insert time*] on [*insert date*]. Please arrange for your representative to be present.

[*Or:*]

Please arrange for your technical representative to telephone to arrange a visit to site in my company in order to suggest solutions to the difficulty.

[*Or:*]

I had intended to use/I have used [*delete as appropriate*] this product on a very large programme of work. Unless I have your proposals to solve the problem in my hands by [*insert date*] I intend to revise my specifying policy.

Yours faithfully

Letter 156

To quantity surveyor regarding defective work
This letter is not suitable for use with CD 81

Dear Sir

The following defective work has been noted on the above site:

[*Insert list of defective work in sufficient detail to enable the quantity surveyor to identify it and include items from previous months until the defects have been corrected*]

The above work is to be omitted from your next valuation.

Yours faithfully

Letter 157

To contractor, if some work included in the application for payment is not in accordance with the contract
This letter is only suitable for use with CD 81

Dear Sir

I am in receipt of your application for payment dated [*insert date*]. I consider that the amount of [*insert amount*] stated as due in your application is not in accordance with the contract. My reasons are set out on the attached schedule which is a notice in accordance with clause 30.3.4 of the conditions of contract. The balance properly due is [*insert amount*] and the employer is sending you a cheque for that sum under separate cover.

[*The schedule should set out that part of the works which the contractor has included in his application, but which are defective or which are not actually carried out, together with the appropriate values to be deducted from the total amount of the application to leave the balance to be paid*]

Yours faithfully

Copy: Employer

Letter 158
To contractor, if defective work opened up

Dear Sir

Together with [*insert name of contractor's representative and clerk of works, if any*], I attended the opening up of [*specify precisely*] at [*insert time*] on [*insert date*].

The work was found to be not in accordance with the contract and an instruction is enclosed under clause 8.4 [*substitute '3.14' when using IFC 84, '31(4)' when using GC/Works/1 or omit the phrase when using MW 80*] requiring removal. The cost of opening up and making good is to be at your expense in accordance with clause 8.3 [*substitute '3.12' when using IFC 84, '31(7)' when using GC/Works/1 or omit the phrase when using MW 80*]. When you consider that the work has been executed in accordance with the contract, the clerk of works/I [*delete as appropriate*] must be allowed to inspect before making good takes place.

Yours faithfully

Copies: Quantity surveyor
Clerk of works [*if appointed*]

Letter 159

To contractor, after failure of work
This letter is only suitable for use with JCT 80 and CD 81

Dear Sir

While visiting site today, I noticed that [*specify work or materials*] were not in accordance with the contract.

In accordance with clause 8.4.4 [*substitute '8.4.3' when using CD 81*] of the conditions of contract and having had due regard to the code of practice appended to such conditions, I enclose my instruction for opening up for inspection/testing [*delete as appropriate*] which is reasonable in all the circumstances to establish to my reasonable satisfaction the likelihood/extent [*delete as appropriate*] of any similar non-compliance.

Yours faithfully

Letter 160

To contractor, after failure of work
This letter is only suitable for use with IFC 84

Dear Sir

While visiting site today, I noted that [*specify work or materials*] were not in accordance with the contract.

In accordance with clause 3.13.1 of the conditions of contract, I require you to state in writing within 7 days of the date of this letter what action you will immediately take at no cost to the employer to establish that there is no similar failure in work already executed/materials or goods already supplied [*delete as appropriate*].

Yours faithfully

Letter 161
To client, confirming instruction which entails extra cost

Dear Sir

I refer to our telephone conversation this morning when you instructed me that the following work was to be carried out: [*specify work*]

I confirm that:

1.   The estimated cost of the work will be [*insert amount*]. The actual amount will be added to the contract sum.
2.   You approve this cost and wish me to instruct the contractor to put the work in hand as soon as possible.

Yours faithfully

Copy: Quantity surveyor

Letter 162
To client, if material change to approved design necessary

Dear Sir

You approved my design for this project on [*insert date*]. Since that time [*insert description of the significant event*]. It is my view that it is necessary to [*describe change in design*] which is a material change from the approved design. This letter is issued in accordance with the Standard Form of Agreement for the Appointment of an Architect paragraph 2.1.3 to confirm that, when we met on [*insert date*], you consented to the change.

Yours faithfully

Letter 163
To contractor, requiring compliance with instruction
Registered Post/Recorded Delivery

Dear Sir

Take this as notice under clause 4.1.2 [*substitute '3.5.1' when using IFC 84, '3.5' when using MW 80 or '53' when using GC/Works/1*] of the conditions of contract that I require you to comply with my instruction number [*insert number*] dated [*insert date*], a further copy of which is enclosed.

If within 7 [*substitute any reasonable period when using GC/Works/1*] days of receipt of this notice you have not complied, the employer may employ and pay others to execute any work necessary to give effect to the instruction. All costs incurred in connection with such employment will be deducted from money due or to become due to you under the contract or will be recovered from you as a debt.

Yours faithfully

Copies: Employer
           Quantity surveyor

Letter 164

To contractor, if he fails to comply with notice
Registered Post/Recorded Delivery

Dear Sir

I refer to the notice issued to you on the *[insert date]* in accordance with clause 4.1.2 *[substitute '3.5.1' when using IFC 84, '3.5' when using MW 80 or '53' when using GC/Works/1]* requiring compliance with my instruction number *[insert number]* dated *[insert date]*.

During a site inspection this morning, I noted that you have not complied with my instruction. The employer is taking immediate steps to employ others to carry out the work. All costs in connection with such employment will be deducted from money due or to become due to you under the contract or will be recovered from you as a debt.

Yours faithfully

Copies: Employer
Quantity surveyor

Letter 165
To contractor, if no grounds for extension of time

Dear Sir

Thank you for your letter of the *[insert date]* in which you asserted that you were entitled to an extension of time for the reasons set out.

On the basis of the documents you have presented to me and of my own knowledge of this project, I can see no grounds for any extension of time. I shall be pleased to consider any further submissions if they are presented in the proper form and in accordance with the terms of the contract.

Yours faithfully

Letter 166
To contractor, if no extension of time due

Dear Sir

I have carefully examined your notice of delay and accompanying particulars and it is my opinion that you are not due to an extension of time/further extension of time [*delete as appropriate*].

Yours faithfully

Letter 167
To contractor, if issuing extension in two parts because of lack of time before completion date

Dear Sir

I have received your delay notices and supporting information on the [*insert date*] and I have now to consider an appropriate extension of time.

In view of the proximity of the contractual completion date and the length of time it will take to consider all aspects of the matter, I enclose an interim extension based upon my initial view of the evidence.

Any further extension of time to which you may be entitled will be given as soon as my investigations are concluded [*substitute 'within the period stipulated in the contract' if appropriate*].

Yours faithfully

Letter 168
To contractor, giving extension of time

Dear Sir

I refer to your notice of delay dated [*insert date and if appropriate, add:*] and the further information provided in your letter dated [*insert date*].

In accordance with clause 25.3 [*substitute '2.3' when using IFC 84, '2.2' when using MW 80 or '36(1)' when using GC/Works/1*] I hereby give you an extension of time of [*insert period*]. The revised date for completion is now [*insert date*].

[*When using JCT 80 or IFC 84, add:*]

The relevant events taken into account are: [*list*]

[*When using JCT 80, add also:*]

[*continued*]

Letter 168 continued

I have had regard to the following instructions requiring as a variation the omission of work:

[*List the instructions and the extent of any reduction in extension of time e.g:*
Architect's Instruction   *Omission from extension*
No. 24, 03.09.95   *14 days*]

[*When using GC/Works/1, add:*]

This is an interim/final [*delete as appropriate*] decision.

Yours faithfully

Letter 169
To client, enclosing a report on extension of time

Dear Sir

The contractor has notified me of likely delay and he has estimated the effect on the completion date.

In making my decision on any entitlement to extension of the contract period, I must act strictly in accordance with the terms of the contract.

I enclose a copy of my brief report on the matter in which I have set out the main factors and my decision in each instance. This report is for your information, but I will be happy to explain anything which may seem unclear.

Yours faithfully

Letter 170

To client, if works not complete by due date and further extensions
may be due
This letter is not suitable for use with MW 80 or GC/Works/1

Dear Sir

The due date for completion of this contract was [*insert date*]
and I enclose my certificate of non-completion as required by
clause 24.1 [*substitute '2.6' when using IFC 84*] of the contract.

You may, if you wish, deduct liquidated damages at the rate
stated in the appendix for the period between the date the
contract should have been completed and the date of practical
completion. Alternatively, you may recover the damages as a
debt. If you decide upon either of these routes, you must first
give the contractor a written requirement, setting out the period
to which the deduction relates and the way in which the damages
are calculated.

Please bear in mind, when deciding whether or not to deduct
liquidated damages, that I have yet to carry out my review of
extensions of time. It is not appropriate to begin until practical
completion has occurred. Further extensions may be due. If, as
a consequence of my review, I fix a later date for completion,
you would be liable to repay any liquidated damages deducted
for the period up to the later completion date.

Yours faithfully

Letter 171a

To contractor, reviewing extensions of time after completion date or
practical completion
This letter is only suitable for use with JCT 80 and CD 81

Dear Sir

I have now completed my consideration of progress in
accordance with clause 25.3.3 of the conditions of contract and

[*Either:*]

I confirm the date of completion of the contract as being [*insert
date*].

[*Or:*]

I hereby give an extension of time of [*insert period*] which
takes into account [*insert relevant events*]. The new date for
completion is [*insert date*].

[*Or:*]

[*continued*]

Letter 171a continued

After having regard to the following instructions [*insert instruction numbers*] requiring omissions and issued after the last occasion on which I made an extension of time, the new date for completion is now [*insert such earlier date as is reasonable but not earlier than the date in the appendix*].

Yours faithfully

Copies: Employer
          Quantity surveyor

Letter 171b

To contractor, reviewing extensions of time after completion date or practical completion
This letter is only suitable for use with IFC 84

Dear Sir

I have now completed my consideration of progress in accordance with clause 2.3 of the conditions of contract and

[*Either:*]

I confirm the date of completion of this contract is [*insert date*].

[*Or:*]

I hereby give an extension of time of [*insert period*] which takes into account [*insert reasons for extension*]. The new date for completion is [*insert date*].

Yours faithfully

Copies: Employer
Quantity surveyor

Letter 172a

To client, enclosing certificate of non-completion
This letter is not suitable for use with MW 80 or GC/Works/1

Dear Sir

I enclose my certificate in accordance with clause 24.1
[*substitute '2.6' when using IFC 84*] of the conditions of
contract.

You may now take steps to recover liquidated damages at the
rate stated in the appendix to the contract. The easiest way to
do this is to deduct the appropriate sum from amounts otherwise
due under my financial certificates. If you decide to follow this
course of action, I enclose a draft letter which you must write to
the contractor before making the deduction so that he is in no
doubt that you intend to make the deduction and the way in
which the amount of the deduction is calculated. You should
inform him in a similar manner before each occasion on which
you intend to deduct liquidated damages.

Yours faithfully

Letter 172b
To client, if works not complete
This letter is only suitable for use with MW 80 or GC/Works/1

Dear Sir

The date for completion/completion date fixed under clause 2.2/completion date fixed under clause 36 [*delete as appropriate*] of the conditions of contract is [*insert date*]. This letter is to inform you that the works are not complete.

You may now take steps to recover liquidated damages at the rate stated in clause 2.3 of the contract [*substitute 'stated in the abstract of particulars' when using GC/Works/1*]. The easiest way to do this is to deduct the appropriate sum from amounts otherwise due under my financial certificates. If you decide to follow this course of action, I enclose a draft letter which you should write to the contractor before making the deduction so that he is in no doubt that you intend to make the deduction and the way in which the amount of the deduction is calculated. You should inform him in a similar manner before each occasion on which you intend to deduct liquidated damages.

Yours faithfully

Letter 173
Draft letter from employer to contractor, before deducting liquidated damages
Registered Post/Recorded Delivery

Dear Sir

In accordance with clause 24.2.1 [*substitute '2.7' when using IFC 84, '2.3' when using MW 80 or '55' when using GC/Works/1*] I require you to pay or allow liquidated damages. I intend to deduct such damages, calculated as follows, from the next financial certificate:

Contract date for completion: [*insert date or extended date*]
Date at which liquidated damages calculated: [*insert date and state if it is also the date of practical completion or completion as appropriate*]
= [*insert number*] weeks @ [*insert amount*] per [*insert unit, e.g, days or weeks*] = [*insert total sum*].

Yours faithfully

Letter 174
To client, advising on the deduction of liquidated damages

Dear Sir

You are entitled to deduct damages at the appropriate rate. The contract stipulates that it is a matter for your discretion alone. Although I am always ready to give you advice, there may be considerations, unknown to me, which will influence your decision.

Yours faithfully

Letter 175

To client, if it would be unfair to deduct liquidated damages

Dear Sir

The due date for completion of this contract was [*insert date*] and the contractor has not yet completed the works/I enclose my certificate of non-completion as required by the contract [*delete as appropriate*].

You are entitled to deduct liquidated damages at the appropriate rate. The decision to deduct is a matter for your discretion alone.

There may be considerations, unknown to me, which will influence your decision. May I, however, draw your attention to the following:

[*Insert any mitigating information on behalf of the contractor*]

You may or may not wish to take this information into account when making your decision.

Yours faithfully

Letter 176

To contractor, giving consent to extension of time for nominated sub-contract
This letter is only suitable for use with JCT 80

Dear Sir

I refer to your notice, particulars and estimate in accordance with clause 35.14 of the contract which I received on the [*insert date*] in respect of the nominated sub-contract works being carried out by [*insert name*].

In accordance with the provisions of clause 35.14 of the contract and clause 2.3 of the sub-contract I hereby give my consent to the extension of time you propose which gives a revised period for completion of the sub-contract works of [*insert period*]. I agree that the matters taken into account in accordance with clause 2.3.3 of the sub-contract are as follows: [*list matters*].

[*If appropriate, add:*]

I further agree that, in giving my consent, I have had regard to the following instructions requiring as variations the omission of work: [*list the instructions and the extent by which they have reduced the period of extension*].

Yours faithfully

Letter 177

To contractor, withholding consent to extension of time for nominated sub-contract
This letter is only suitable for use with JCT 80

Dear Sir

I refer to your notice, particulars and estimate submitted under the provisions of clause 35.14 of the contract which I received on the [*insert date*] in respect of the nominated sub-contract works carried out by [*insert name*].

I cannot give my consent to your proposed award of extension of time, because I consider the period is not correct.

Yours faithfully

Letter 178
To contractor, withholding certificate of nominated sub-contractor's failure to complete
This letter is only suitable for use with JCT 80

Dear Sir

I refer to your notice dated [*insert date*] and submitted under clause 35.15.1 of the contract.

I decline to issue my certificate that [*insert name of nominated sub-contractor*] has failed to complete the sub-contract works within the period specified in the sub-contract/the extended time granted with my written consent [*delete as appropriate*], because

[*Insert either:*]

I am not satisfied that [*insert name of nominated sub-contractor*] has so failed.

[*Or:*]

I am not satisfied that clause 35.14 has been properly applied.

Yours faithfully

Letter 179
To contractor, certifying nominated sub-contractor's failure to complete
This letter is only suitable for use with JCT 80

Dear Sir

I refer to your notice dated [*insert date*] and submitted under clause 35.15.1 of the contract.

I certify that [*insert name of nominated sub-contractor*] of [*insert address*] has failed to complete the sub-contract works within the period specified in the sub-contract/the extended time granted by the contractor with my written consent [*delete as appropriate*] namely [*insert period*].

Yours faithfully

Copy: Nominated sub-contractor

Letter 180

To client, regarding common law claims
This letter is not suitable for use with MW 80

Dear Sir

I enclose an application for additional payment dated [*insert date*] sent to me by the main contractor.

The contract makes provisions for me to deal with financial claims of specific kinds. This application does not/parts of this application do not [*delete as appropriate*] fall within these provisions and I have no authority under the contract to ascertain either validity or payment.

I advise that you should not simply reject the claim at this stage, because the contractor may decide to pursue the matter through the courts or in arbitration. If you give me the requisite authority, I am prepared to examine the application on its merits and advise you regarding payment. Alternatively, you may wish to obtain specialised advice from a solicitor or other person versed in construction law. If so, I should be happy to accompany you to provide any additional information required.

Yours faithfully

Letter 181
To client regarding loss and/or expense applications
This letter is only suitable for use with MW 80

Dear Sir

I enclose an application for loss and/or expense dated [*insert date*] which has been submitted by the main contractor. Although there is a limited provision in clause 3.6 for me to include direct loss and/or expense in the valuation of instructions, the contract provisions do not allow me to ascertain validity or payment for submissions such as the enclosed.

Do not reject the claim out of hand, because the contractor may decide to pursue his claim through the courts or in arbitration, which could be expensive. If you wish to discuss the claim with me, please telephone to arrange a suitable time for a meeting. It may be possible to settle the matter quite easily with the contractor. At our meeting, we could discuss whether it is necessary to obtain specialised advice before proceeding.

Yours faithfully

Letter 182
To client, regarding ex-gratia claims

Dear Sir

I enclose an application for payment dated [*insert date*] sent to me by the main contractor.

The claim appears to be purely ex gratia. In other words, it has no legal basis. The contractor is simply asking you to consider making a payment, because he has suffered hardship. Let me know if you require any particular information in order to come to a decision. Remember that, even if you decide that the contractor has indeed suffered hardship, you are under no obligation to pay anything.

Yours faithfully

Letter 183

To contractor, if ex-gratia or common law application submitted

Dear Sir

I have received your application for payment dated [*insert date*] which has been passed to the employer for his decision, because it does not fall within the limits of my authority under the terms of the contract.

Yours faithfully

Copies: Employer
Quantity surveyor

Letter 184

To contractor, rejecting application due to failure to comply with contract
This letter is not suitable for use with MW 80

Dear Sir

I refer to your application for loss and/or expense [*substitute 'expense' when using GC/Works/1*] received on the [*insert date*].

I cannot begin to consider your claim, because you have failed to comply with the requirements of clause 26 [*substitute '4.11' when using IFC 84 or '46' when using GC/Works/1*]. In particular, you have failed in your duty to [*specify, clearly and concisely, how the contractor has failed*].

Yours faithfully

Copy: Quantity surveyor

Letter 185

To contractor, if application badly presented
This letter is not suitable for use with MW 80

Dear Sir

I refer to your application for loss and/or expense [*substitute
'expense' when using GC/Works/1*] dated [*insert date*].

Although it appears, at first sight, that you have satisfied all the
procedural requirements of the contract and I can begin to
consider your application, the presentation is confusing. I am
prepared to examine the application as it stands, but I must warn
you that it is my duty to reject it, or any part of it, if I am not
satisfied of its validity.

Please consider whether you wish to resubmit your application in
a more comprehensible form. I will postpone my consideration
for seven days to give you the opportunity to decide. If you
think that a short meeting would clarify the situation, I am
prepared to arrange it if you will telephone to agree a suitable
day and time.

Yours faithfully

Copy: Quantity surveyor

Letter 186
To contractor, after receipt of estimate under the supplementary provisions
This letter is only suitable for use with CD 81

Dear Sir

I refer to your estimate of the addition to the contract sum, which you require in respect of direct loss and/or expense, submitted with your application for interim payment dated [*insert date*].

[*Either*]

I accept your estimate.

[*Or:*]

I wish to negotiate on the amount of the addition to the contract sum and in default of agreement to refer the issue for decision by the adjudicator under S1.

[*Or:*]

I wish to negotiate on the amount of the addition to the contract sum and in default of agreement the provisions of clause 26 shall apply.

[*continued*]

Letter 186 continued

[*Or:*]

The provisions of clause 26 shall apply in respect of the loss and/or expense to which the estimate relates.

Yours faithfully

Letter 187
To contractor, requesting further information in support of financial claim
This letter is not suitable for use with MW 80

Dear Sir

I refer to your application for loss and/or expense [*substitute 'expense' when using GC/Works/1*] dated [*insert date and add, if appropriate:*] and the further particulars which I received on the [*insert date*].

In accordance with clause 26.1 [*substitute 'S7.4' when using supplementary provisions of CD 81, '4.11' when using IFC 84 or '46(3)(b)' when using GC/Works/1*] I require the following information before I can begin to consider your application:

[*Insert brief details of information required*]

Yours faithfully

Copy: Quantity surveyor

Letter 188

To contractor, rejecting application for loss and/or expense
This letter is not suitable for use with MW 80

Dear Sir

I refer to your application for loss and/or expense [*substitute
'expense' when using GC/Works/1*], under clause 26 [*substitute
'4.11' when using IFC 84 or '46' when using GC/Works/1*] of
the contract, received on the [*insert date*].

After careful consideration of the evidence, I have to inform you
that I can find no grounds for ascertaining any loss and/or
expense [*substitute 'expense' when using GC/Works/1*] at this
time.

Yours faithfully

Copy: Quantity surveyor

Letter 189

To contractor, accepting financial claim
This letter is not suitable for use with MW 80

Dear Sir

I refer to your application for loss and/or expense [*substitute
'expense' when using GC/Works/1*], the last part of which I
received on [*insert date*].

I have carefully considered the evidence and I am of the opinion
that there is some merit in your application. Therefore, I am
proceeding/I am asking the quantity surveyor [*delete as
appropriate*] to ascertain the amount to be added to the contract
sum.

[*Add, when using JCT 80, if appropriate:*]

In carrying out the ascertainment, regard will be made to the
following extensions of time made under the provisions of clause
25:

[*List relevant events and periods of extension*].

Yours faithfully

Letter 190

To quantity surveyor, requesting ascertainment of loss and/or expense
This letter is not suitable for use with MW 80

Dear Sir

I enclose an application dated [*insert date*] received from the contractor in respect of loss and/or expense [*substitute 'expense' when using GC/Works/1*].

In my opinion, the application is properly made and discloses a valid entitlement. I should be pleased if you would proceed as soon as possible to ascertain the payment due to the contractor.

Yours faithfully

Letter 191

To client, enclosing report on application
This letter is not suitable for use with MW 80

Dear Sir

I have received an application from the contractor in which he asks for payment of loss and/or expense caused by [*insert matters briefly*].

In making my decision on any entitlement to payment, I must act strictly in accordance with the terms of the contract.

I enclose a copy of my brief report setting out the main points of the application and my decisions in each case. This report is for your information, but I will be happy to explain anything which may seem unclear.

Yours faithfully

Letter 192
To consultants, regarding testing and commissioning of plant

Dear Sir

Your programmed dates for testing and commissioning of [*insert nature of plant*] are [*insert dates*]. Please let me know by return if these dates are still valid so that I can invite the client to be present.

Yours faithfully

Letter 193

To client, regarding testing and commissioning of plant

Dear Sir

Arrangements have been made for the [*insert nature of plant*] to be tested and commissioned on the [*insert dates*] beginning at [*insert time*]. It would be advisable for you or your representative to be present to witness the procedure and to satisfy yourself with regard to the operation of the plant.

Yours faithfully

Copies: Consultants
Clerk of works

Letter 194a

To contractor, giving notice of default
This letter is only suitable for use with JCT 80 and CD 81
Registered Post/Recorded Delivery

Dear Sir

I hereby give you notice under clause 27.2 of the conditions of contract that you are in default in the following respects:

[Insert details of the default with dates if appropriate]

If you continue the default for fourteen days after receipt of this notice or if at any time you repeat such default, whether previously repeated or not, the employer may within ten days of such continuance or repetition forthwith determine your employment under this contract without further notice.

Yours faithfully

Copies: Employer
Quantity surveyor

Letter 194b
To contractor, giving notice of default
This letter is only suitable for use with IFC 84
Registered Post/Recorded Delivery

Dear Sir

I hereby give notice under clause 7.1 of the contract that you are in default in the following respects:

[Insert details of the default with dates if appropriate]

If you continue the default for fourteen days after receipt of this notice or if at any time you repeat such default, whether previously repeated or not, the employer may thereupon determine your employment under this contract without further notice.

Yours faithfully

Copies: Employer
　　　　Quantity surveyor

Letter 194c
To contractor, giving notice of default
This letter is only suitable for use with MW 80
Registered Post/Recorded Delivery

Dear Sir

I hereby give notice under clause 7.2.1 of the contract that you
are in default in the following respects:

[*Insert details of the default with dates if appropriate*]

If you continue the default for seven days after receipt of this
notice, the employer may thereupon determine your employment
under this contract without further notice.

Yours faithfully

Copies: Employer
            Quantity surveyor [*if appointed*]

Letter 195a
To client, if contractor continues his default
This letter is only suitable for use with JCT 80 or CD 81

Dear Sir

I refer to our conversation on the [*insert date*] following which I sent a notice of default to the contractor.

I carried out a site inspection this morning in company with the clerk of works and I have to report that [*insert details of the default*] is continuing. Under the terms of the contract and specifically clause 27.2.2 you may, if you so wish, determine the employment of the contractor forthwith and I enclose a draft letter which you should use for that purpose. I anticipate that you will wish to discuss the matter with me before taking any further action and I will telephone you tomorrow.

Please note that if you decide to determine the contractor's employment, you must do so by [*insert date*] at the latest.

Yours faithfully

Letter 195b
To client, if contractor continues his default
This letter is only suitable for use with IFC 84 or MW 80

Dear Sir

I refer to our conversation on the [*insert date*] following which I sent a notice of default to the contractor.

I carried out a site inspection this morning in company with the clerk of works and I have to report that [*insert details of the default*] is continuing. Under the terms of the contract and specifically clause 7.1 [*substitute '7.2.1' when using MW 80*] you may, if you so wish, determine the employment of the contractor forthwith and I enclose a draft letter which you should use for that purpose. I anticipate that you will wish to discuss the matter with me before taking any further action and I will telephone you tomorrow.

Please note that if you decide to determine the contractor's employment, you must not delay in taking action.

Yours faithfully

Letter 195c
To client, if contractor is in default
This letter is only suitable for use with GC/Works/1

Dear Sir

I refer to our conversation on the [*insert date*] when we discussed [*insert brief details of the contractor's default*].

I carried out a site inspection this morning in company with the clerk of works and I have to report that [*insert details of the default*] is continuing. The situation is clearly very serious and I believe that the contractor is making little effort to rectify matters. Under the terms of the contract and specifically clause 56 you may, if you so wish, determine the contract forthwith and I enclose a draft letter which you could use for that purpose. I anticipate that you will wish to discuss the matter with me before taking any further action and I will telephone you tomorrow.

Yours faithfully

Letter 195d

To client, if determination under 28A possible
This letter is only suitable for use with JCT 80 or CD 81
Registered Post/Recorded Delivery

Dear Sir

On the [*insert date*] the whole or substantially the whole of the
works will have been suspended for [*insert period stated in the
appendix*]. Immediately thereafter, you may issue a notice that
unless the suspension is terminated within 7 days of receipt of
the notice, the contractor's employment under the contract will
determine. This is an extremely serious step and if you wish I
can draft you an appropriate notice. However, I suggest that we
should meet to discuss the possible consequences in detail. I will
telephone you in the next few days.

Yours faithfully

Letter 195e
To client, if determination under clause 7.8.1 possible
This letter is only suitable for use with IFC 84
Registered Post/Recorded Delivery

Dear Sir

On the *[insert date]* the whole or substantially the whole of the works will have been suspended for three months. Immediately thereafter, you may issue a notice forthwith determining the contractor's employment under the contract. This is an extremely serious step and if you wish I can draft you an appropriate notice. However, I suggest that we should meet to discuss the possible consequences in detail. I will telephone you in the next few days.

Yours faithfully

Letter 196a

Draft letter from employer to contractor, determining employment
This letter is only suitable for use with JCT 80 or CD 81
Registered Post/Recorded Delivery

Dear Sir

I refer to the notice dated [*insert date of notice*] sent to you by the architect.

In accordance with clause 27.2.2 of the contract take this as notice that I hereby forthwith determine your employment under this contract without prejudice to any other rights or remedies which I may possess.

The rights and duties of the parties are governed by clauses 27.6 and 27.7. No temporary buildings, plant, tools, equipment, goods or materials shall be removed from site until and if the architect shall so instruct.

The architect will write to you within fourteen days regarding all sub-contractors and suppliers [*when using JCT 80, add:*] whether nominated or otherwise.

Yours faithfully

Copies: Architect
         Quantity surveyor

Letter 196b
Draft letter from employer to contractor, determining employment
after loss or damage
This letter is not suitable for use with MW 80 or GC/Works/1
Registered Post/Recorded Delivery

Dear Sir

I refer to your notice of the *[insert date]* giving notice of loss or
damage occasioned by *[insert particulars of loss or damage
which must have been occasioned by one or more of the insured
risks]*.

In accordance with clause 22C.4.3.1 *[substitute '6.3C.4.3' when
using IFC 84]* take this as notice that I hereby forthwith
determine your employment under the contract, because I
consider that it is just and equitable so to do.

The rights and duties of the parties are governed by clause
22C.4.3.2 *[substitute '6.3C.4.3' when using IFC 84]*.

Yours faithfully

Copies: Architect
Quantity surveyor

Letter 196c

Draft letter from employer to contractor, determining employment
This letter is only suitable for use with IFC 84
Registered Post/Recorded Delivery

Dear Sir

I refer to the notice dated [*insert date of notice*] sent to you by the architect.

In accordance with clause 7.1 of the contract take this as notice that I hereby forthwith determine your employment under this contract without prejudice to any other rights or remedies which I may possess.

The rights and duties of the parties are governed by clauses 7.4. The architect will write to you within the next seven days with instructions regarding the temporary buildings, plant, tools, equipment, goods and materials on site. Subject only to your compliance with the architect's instructions, you must give up possession of the site forthwith.

Yours faithfully

Copies: Architect
　　　　　Quantity surveyor

Letter 196d
Draft letter from employer to contractor, determining employment
under clause 28A
This letter is only suitable for use with JCT 80 or CD 81
Registered Post/Recorded Delivery

Dear Sir

The whole or substantially the whole of the works has been
suspended since [*insert date*], a period of [*insert length stated in
the appendix*], by reason of [*insert reason for suspension*].

In accordance with clause 28A.1.1 of the contract, take this as
notice that unless the suspension is terminated within 7 days of
the date of receipt of this notice, your employment under this
contract will determine 7 days after receipt of this notice.

The rights and duties of the parties are governed by clauses
28A.3 to 28A.6 [*substitute '28A.3 to 28A.7' when using CD 81*].
I will draw up a statement of account as soon as reasonably
practicable.

Yours faithfully

Copies: Architect
Quantity surveyor

Letter 196e
Draft letter from employer to contractor, determining employment
under clause 7.8.1
This letter is only suitable for use with IFC 84
Registered Post/Recorded Delivery

Dear Sir

The whole or substantially the whole of the works has been
suspended since [*insert date*], a period of three months, by
reason of [*insert reason for suspension*].

In accordance with clause 7.8.1 of the contract, take this as
notice that I hereby forthwith determine your employment under
this contract without prejudice to any other rights or remedies
which I may possess.

The rights and duties of the parties are governed by clause 7.9.
The architect will draw up a statement of account as soon as
reasonably practicable.

Yours faithfully

Copies: Architect
          Quantity surveyor

Letter 196f
Draft letter from employer to contractor, determining employment
This letter is only suitable for use with MW 80
Registered Post/Recorded Delivery

Dear Sir

I refer to the notice dated [*insert date of notice*] sent to you by
the architect.

In accordance with clause 7.2.1 of the contract take this as notice
that I hereby forthwith determine your employment under this
contract without prejudice to any other rights or remedies which
I may possess.

You must immediately give up possession of the site.

The rights and duties of the parties are governed by clause 7.3.
Take note that I am not bound to make any further payments to
you until after completion of the works and the making good of
any defects therein. I reserve any rights to that time.

Yours faithfully

Copies: Architect
Quantity surveyor [*if appointed*]

Letter 196g
Draft letter from employer to contractor, determining contract
This letter is only suitable for use with GC/Works/1
Registered Post/Recorded Delivery

Dear Sir

Take this as notice under clause 56(1) of the contract that I hereby determine this contract.

[*If appropriate add:*]

The following grounds apply: [*describe any grounds which fall within clause 56(6)*]

[*Then:*]

The rights of the parties are governed by clause 57/58 [*delete as appropriate*]. I will write to you as soon as practicable, but in any event not later than three months hence/the date of completion [*delete whichever is later*] to give directions under clause 56(3). You must not remove any Things of whatsoever kind before you receive my directions.

Yours faithfully

Copies: Architect
Quantity surveyor

Letter 197
To client, regarding insurance after determination

Dear Sir

Your notice of determination is being sent to the contractor today. The contractor no longer has any liability to insure the works. You should consult your own broker without delay to obtain cover similar to that which the contractor was required to have under the provisions of this contract. I enclose copies of clauses 20 to 22A [*substitute '6.1 to 6.3' when using IFC 84 or MW 80 or '8' when using GC/Works/1*] which you should give to your broker.

Your insurance cover should be maintained at least until suitable arrangements have been made to complete the works using another contractor.

Yours faithfully

Copy: Quantity surveyor

Letter 198

To client, if contractor likely to determine his employment under the contract
This letter is not suitable for use with GC/Works/1

Dear Sir

I have reason to believe that the contractor is seriously considering taking action to determine his employment under the contract.

The results of such action would be disastrous for the project in terms of time and money and I have arranged a special meeting with the contractor at this office to hear his grievances. The meeting will be at [*insert time*] on [*insert date*] and I should be grateful if you would keep yourself available to approve any action which may need to be taken. In any event, I will telephone immediately after the meeting to inform you of the result.

Yours faithfully

Letter 199

To client, if contractor determines his employment
This letter is not suitable for use with GC/Works/1

Dear Sir

I understand that the contractor has today sent notice
determining his employment under the contract.

The result of this action could be very serious and you should
take specialist advice as a matter of urgency. I will accompany
you at the meeting together with the quantity surveyor in order
to provide any information that may be required. We will make
ourselves available at any time.

Yours faithfully

Copy: Quantity surveyor

Letter 200
Draft letter from employer to contractor, requesting adjudication
This letter is only suitable for use with CD 81
Registered Post/Recorded Delivery

Dear Sir

A dispute of difference as referred to in supplementary provision
S1.1 has arisen in that [*give brief details of the dispute*].

Take this as notice required under supplementary provision
S1.3.1. Within 14 days of the date of this notice, I shall set out
the matters in dispute in statements to the adjudicator named in
appendix 1.

Yours faithfully

Copy: Adjudicator

Letter 201
Draft letter from employer to contractor, if adjudicator's decision
unacceptable
This letter is only suitable for use with CD 81
Registered Post/Recorded Delivery

Dear Sir

I received the adjudicator's decision on [*insert date*] and such
decision is not acceptable. This notice is given under
supplementary provision S1.3.4.

I request you to concur in the appointment of an arbitrator
under article 5 and clause 39 of the conditions of contract and I
suggest the following three persons for your consideration. Your
concurrence is required within 14 days of the date of this notice,
failing which I shall apply to the appointor named in appendix 1.

[*List the names and addresses of the three persons*]

Yours faithfully

Letter 202

Draft letter from employer to contractor, requesting concurrence in the appointment of an arbitrator
Registered Post/Recorded Delivery

Dear Sir

I hereby give you notice that I require the undermentioned dispute or difference between us to be referred to arbitration in accordance with article 5 and clause 41   [*substitute 'article 5 and clause 39' when using CD 81, 'article 5 and clause 9' when using IFC 84, 'article 4 and clause 9' when using MW 80 or 'clause 60' when using GC/Works/1*] of the contract between us dated [*insert date*]. Please treat this as a request to concur in the appointment of an arbitrator.

The dispute or difference is [*insert brief description*]

I propose the following three persons for your consideration and require your concurrence in the appointment within 14 days of the date of service of this letter, failing which I shall apply to the President or Vice-President of the Royal Institute of British Architects/Royal Institution of Chartered Surveyors/Chartered Institute of Arbitrators/Law Society/Law Society of Scotland/Institution of Civil Engineers [*delete as appropriate*].

[*List names and addresses of the three persons*]

Yours faithfully

Letter 203

Draft letter from employer to professional body if there is no
concurrence in the appointment of an arbitrator

Dear Sir

I am an employer who has entered into a building contract in
JCT 80 form, clause 41.1 [*substitute 'CD 81 form, clause 39.1',
'IFC 84 form, clause 9.1', 'MW 80 form, clause 9.1' or
'GC/Works/1 form, clause 60(1)' as appropriate*] which makes
provision for your President or Vice-President to appoint an
arbitrator in default of agreement.

I should be pleased to receive an appropriate form of application
and supporting documentation, together with a note of the
current fee payable on application.

Yours faithfully

Letter 204

To client, if impractical to carry out certain services
Registered Post/Recorded Delivery

Dear Sir

In accordance with clause 1.6.1 of the RIBA Standard Form of
Agreement for the Appointment of an Architect 1992, I am
required to give you this notice that a circumstance has arisen,
namely [*insert concise details*], which make it impracticable to
carry out [*insert details of services*].

I should be grateful, therefore, if you would telephone me as a
matter of urgency in order to agree a suitable course of action
having regard to all the circumstances.

Yours faithfully

Letter 205

To client, terminating appointment by reasonable notice
Registered Post/Recorded Delivery

Dear Sir

In accordance with clause 1.6.5 of the RIBA Standard Form of
Agreement for the Appointment of an Architect 1992, please
take this as notice that I intend to terminate my appointment as
architect for the project on the [*insert date of termination, which
must be reasonable having regard to the size and complexity of
the project and the stage reached*].

I shall be happy to meet you to discuss matters arising from this
termination, including the use of drawings and documents
already prepared, my fees and the appointment of another
architect. Please inform me of a date and time which will be
convenient for you to attend this office or alternatively, if you
prefer, for me to visit you.

Yours faithfully

Letter 206

To client, if client terminates appointment by reasonable notice
Registered Post/Recorded Delivery

Dear Sir

Thank you for your letter of the [*insert date*], by which I understand that you intend to terminate my appointment as architect for the above project on the [*insert date*].

I am arranging to cease my work on the date stated and immediately thereafter I will submit an account to cover all outstanding fees. When I receive your payment, you will be entitled to all the drawings and documents prepared for the work although, in view of the circumstances, the information will be incomplete and I cannot accept responsibility for errors or omissions.

[*If stage D has been completed or if you are charged full fees, add:*]

You are entitled to reproduce the design on the site to which it relates. The copyright in all drawings and documents remains my property.

[*continued*]

Letter 206 continued

[If stage D has not been completed or if you are charging a nominal fee, add instead:]

You are not entitled to reproduce my designs by executing the project without my permission. I am prepared to grant you permission to reproduce my design on the site to which it relates on payment of an additional fee of *[insert amount]*. The copyright in all the documents remains my property.

Yours faithfully

Letter 207

To client, if client has not given instructions to resume suspended service within six months
Registered Post/Recorded Delivery

Dear Sir

You suspended my services in connection with the above project by your notice of the [*insert date*]. The effective date of suspension of services was [*insert date*].

It is now more than six months from the date of suspension and, in accordance with clause 1.6.4 of the RIBA Standard Form of Agreement for the Appointment of an Architect 1992, I hereby make written request for instructions to resume my services, such instructions to be in writing.

If such instructions have not been received by me within 28 days of the date of this letter, I have the right to treat the appointment as terminated.

Yours faithfully

Letter 208

To client, if another architect appointed
Registered Post/Recorded Delivery

Dear Sir

I was surprised to hear that you have appointed another architect to carry out the above project. Perhaps you would be good enough to confirm that my information is correct?

My own appointment, of course, continues until you formally give me reasonable notice of termination in accordance with clause 1.6.5 of the RIBA Standard Form of Agreement for the Appointment of an Architect 1992. I should be pleased to hear from you on this matter so I can take appropriate action, including stopping work, closing my files and preparing my fee account.

Yours faithfully

Letter 209
To other architect, appointed by client
Registered Post/Recorded Delivery

Dear Sir

I have been informed that my client [*insert name*] has instructed you to carry out work on the above project. Since I have not had any communication from you in accordance with principle 3, rule 3.5 of the **RIBA Code of Professional Conduct**, I should be pleased if you would let me know if my information is correct.

Clearly, you were not aware of my prior involvement, but I suggest that if you have accepted my client's instructions, you should inform him that it would not be proper for you to proceed until the appropriate termination formalities, including payment of my fees, have been completed.

I have written to my client informing him of the necessity of terminating my appointment in strict accordance with the applicable conditions of the **RIBA Standard Form of Agreement for the Appointment of an Architect 1992**.

Yours faithfully

11 Completion

These letters deal with the preparation for inspection prior to completion, the defects liability period and some matters before the issue of the final certificate.

Examples of certificates have not been given, because purpose-printed forms are readily available.

Letter 210

To client, if client wishes to use new building before completion certified

Dear Sir

I understand that you wish to use the building/part of the building [*delete as appropriate*] before I certify practical completion [*substitute 'that the works are completed to my satisfaction' when using GC/Works/1*].

I strongly advise you not to follow this course of action, because it may give rise to complications. If it is absolutely essential that you use the building, the contractor may well assert that such use has caused damage for which he will hold you liable. Such assertions are always difficult to refute completely.

It is a matter for you to decide and let me have your instructions. The contractor's permission must be obtained and there are insurance implications to discuss with your insurance broker.

Yours faithfully

Letter 211
To client, prior to completion

Dear Sir

I anticipate that the building will be ready for you to take possession on [*insert date*] and I intend to arrange a meeting with the contractor so that you can accept the keys on that date. If you will provisionally reserve the afternoon of that day, I will confirm arrangements as soon as I am satisfied that there are unlikely to be any last minute hitches.

The contractor's insurance obligations will cease on handover and you should make arrangements for full insurance cover effective from [*insert date*]. In order to assist you, I estimate the building value at [*insert amount*], but you should consult your insurance broker regarding the need to ensure that your insurance includes all rebuilding costs and professional fees.

Yours faithfully

Copy: Clerk of works

Letter 212
To client, confirming handover meeting

Dear Sir

I refer to my letter of the [*insert date*] in which I said that I expected to be able to hold a handover meeting in the afternoon of [*insert date*].

[*Add, if date confirmed:*]

I am pleased to be able to confirm this arrangement and I propose collecting you at [*insert time and any further matters, such as lunch, which you have to settle*].

[*Add, if date changed:*]

Unfortunately certain important parts of the work will be unfinished on that day and I, therefore, suggest [*insert date*] for the handover meeting. If this is convenient, I propose collecting you at [*insert time and any further matters, such as lunch, which you have to settle*].

[*Then:*]

Please let me know that the date and time are convenient.

Yours faithfully

Letter 213

To contractor, regarding inspection before completion

Dear Sir

I propose to visit site on [*insert date*] to carry out a full inspection of the works before the handover meeting on the [*insert date*] at which the client will be present.

All consultants will be in attendance and I should be pleased if you would arrange to have everything ready, all keys available and [*insert name of contractor's representative*] on hand.

Yours faithfully

Copies: Quantity surveyor
Consultants
Clerk of works

Letter 214
To consultants, regarding inspection before completion

Dear Sir

I enclose a copy of my letter to the contractor which is self-explanatory.

Please confirm that you will be present at the meeting.

Yours faithfully

Letter 215
To client, after handover

Dear Sir

I refer to the handover meeting held on site at the above project
at which [*list names and firms*] were present. I confirm that
after an inspection of the building you expressed yourself
generally satisfied and accepted [*insert detailed list of all keys,
documents, etc, accepted*]. Your own insurance should now be
effective. If your broker has not confirmed it, press him to
confirm without delay.

The defects liability [*substitute 'maintenance' when using
GC/Works/1*] period extends from the date of practical
completion [*substitute 'completion to my satisfaction' when using
GC/Works/1*] to [*insert date*]. Although I will make my own
inspection during this period, it would be helpful if you would
make a note of any defects which you notice so that I can
include them on my list. If any defects become apparent and
cause you any inconvenience, please let me know so that I can
instruct the contractor to attend to them immediately.

Yours faithfully

Letter 216
To contractor, if sending schedule of defects

Dear Sir

The defects liability [*substitute ' maintenance' when using GC/Works/1*] period ended on the [*insert date*]. In accordance with clause 17.2 [*substitute '16.2' when using CD 81, '2.10' when using IFC 84, '2.5' when using MW 80 or '21' when using GC/Works/1*] of the contract I enclose a schedule of the defects I found during my inspection carried out on the [*insert date*]. I should be pleased if you would give your immediate attention to these defects.

Yours faithfully

Copy: Clerk of works

Letter 217

To contractor, if immediate attention required during the defects
liability period
This letter is only suitable for use with JCT 80 or CD 81

Dear Sir

Notwithstanding the provisions of clause 17.2 [*substitute '16.2'
when using CD 81*] of the contract, clause 17.3 [*substitute '16.3'
when using CD 81*] empowers me to issue instructions regarding
the making good of defects whenever I consider it necessary to
do so.

The enclosed instruction refers to making good which falls into
this category and I should be pleased if you would carry out the
instruction forthwith.

Yours faithfully

Copy: Clerk of works

Letter 218

To contractor, requiring making good during the defects liability/ maintenance period

Dear Sir

As a matter of urgency, please carry out making good as indicated on the enclosed instruction.

The instruction is issued in accordance with clause 17.3 [*substitute '16.3' when using CD 81, '2.10' when using IFC 84, '2.5' when using MW 80 or '21' when using GC/Works/1*]

Yours faithfully

Copy: Clerk of works

Letter 219
To client, if some defects are not to be made good
This letter is not suitable for use with GC/Works/1

Dear Sir

I understand that you do not require the contractor to make good the following defects: [*list*].

These defects are included in my schedule of defects issued to the contractor at the end of the defects liability period. In order that I may issue the appropriate instructions I should be pleased if you would confirm the following:

1.   You do not require the contractor to carry out making good to the defects listed in this letter.
2.   You authorise me to make an appropriate deduction from the contract sum.
3.   You waive any rights you may have against any persons in regard to the items listed as defects in the above-mentioned schedule of defects and not made good.
4.   You agree to indemnify me against any claims made by third parties in respect of such defects.

Yours faithfully

Letter 220

To contractor, instructing that some defects are not to be made good
This letter is not suitable for use with GC/Works/1

Dear Sir

The defects liability period ended on the [*insert date*]. I
inspected the works on the [*insert date*] and enclosed is a
schedule of the defects found.

I hereby instruct that, in accordance with clause 17.2
[*substitute'16.2' when using CD 81, '2.10' when using IFC 84 or
'2.5' when using MW 80*], you are not required to make good any
of the defects shown on the schedule/those defects marked 'E'
[*delete as appropriate*].

An appropriate deduction will be made from the contract sum in
respect of the defects which you are not required to make good.

Yours faithfully

Copies: Employer
           Quantity surveyor
           Clerk of works

Letter 221
To contractor, requiring 'as-built' records

Dear Sir

A complete and accurate record of the building as built is essential for the employer's future maintenance procedures. Such records are required in the contract documents [*indicate position in bills of quantities or specification by stating the appropriate page numbers and references, refer to 'clause 5.5' when using CD 81 if the records were not received before the commencement of the defects liability period*].

Depending on the extent of your own records, you may be involved in contacting the appropriate sub-contractors and taking additional measurements. I must stress that completeness and accuracy of such records is entirely your responsibility.

Please inform me, during the next week, when I can expect to receive a full set of as-built records.

Yours faithfully

Letter 222

To contractor, requiring return of all drawings and documents
This letter is only suitable for use with JCT 80

Dear Sir

In accordance with clause 5.6 of the contract I formally request you to return to me all drawings, details, descriptive schedules, bills of quantities or specification or other like documents which bear my name.

Yours faithfully

Letter 223

To contractor, requiring return of all drawings and documents

Dear Sir

Please return to me all drawings, details, schedules and other like documents which bear my name.

The documents are my copyright and neither they nor the information they contain may be used for any purpose whatsoever without my express written permission.

Yours faithfully

Copies: Employer
Quantity surveyor
Consultants
Clerk of works

12 Feedback

Architects seem to be divided about the wisdom of inviting feedback at the conclusion of a project. Most agree that it is a good thing in the abstract, but few put it into practice in a whole-hearted way. Most of the reluctance is apparently centred on the fear that the client may use your efforts at obtaining feedback to voice his complaints. In view of the ever-present threat of litigation, it is not surprising. Letters 227 and 228 deal with the situation if latent defects become apparent.

Letter 224

To client, requesting feedback information

Dear Sir

I always endeavour to carry out a feedback exercise after the building has been in use for a few months. I have found it useful for resolving any problems which may present themselves and to assist in refining my procedures for future work.

I am arranging a meeting with members of the design team and I should be grateful if you could let me have some dates on which you would be free to attend.

Among the subjects for discussion will be the effectiveness of communication procedures throughout all stages of the work and the satisfactory operation of the finished building.

Yours faithfully

Letter 225
To consultants, requesting feedback information

Dear Sir

I always endeavour to carry out a feedback exercise after the building has been in use for a few months. I have found it useful for resolving any problems which may present themselves and to assist in improving procedures to our mutual benefit. This could be especially useful in the event of future work together.

I am arranging a meeting with all the members of the design team and I have invited the client to attend and to contribute to the discussion.

Among subjects for discussion will be the effectiveness of communication procedures throughout all stages of the work and the satisfactory operation of the finished building.

I should be grateful if you would let me have some dates on which you are free to attend.

Yours faithfully

Letter 226
To contractor, requesting feedback information

Dear Sir

I always endeavour to carry out a feedback exercise after the building has been in use for a few months. I have found it useful for resolving any problems which may present themselves and to assist in improving procedures to our mutual benefit. This could be especially useful in the event of future work together.

I am arranging a meeting with all the members of the design team and I should be grateful if you would let me have some dates on which you are free to attend.

Among subjects for discussion will be the effectiveness of communication procedures throughout all stages of the work and the satisfactory operation of the finished building.

Yours faithfully

Letter 227
To client, regarding latent defects

Dear Sir

Following your telephone call of the [*insert date*], I inspected
[*describe*] today and I noted that [*briefly describe the visual
appearance of the defect*]. It is difficult to establish the cause
with any certainty until a detailed investigation has been carried
out.

[*If there is any possibility that the limitation period for the defect
may expire add:*]

The limitation period in respect of this problem may soon expire.
In order to safeguard your rights, I strongly urge you to seek
legal advice on the point immediately. It is not possible for me
to take a view on liability at this stage, but the original
contractor should be involved. If you wish me to carry out a
detailed investigation, I would be happy to assist and a copy of
the RIBA Standard Form of Agreement for the Appointment of
an Architect 1992, together with details of my fees and expenses
are enclosed for your information.

[*continued*]

Letter 227 continued

[*Otherwise, add:*]

The original contractor should be involved. I shall be happy to deal with this matter if you wish and a copy of the RIBA Standard Form of Agreement for the Appointment of an Architect 1992, together with details of my fees and expenses are enclosed for your information.

Yours faithfully

Letter 228
To contractor, regarding latent defects

Dear Sir

My client asked me to inspect a defect in the above works which became apparent on or about [*insert date*]. The problem appears to be [*briefly describe the defect*].

I have carried out a preliminary inspection and my opinion is that the defect is your responsibility. Please telephone me during the week in order to arrange a joint inspection.

Yours faithfully

Index